The Dynamics of Emerging De-Facto States

What are the causes and consequences of the crisis in Ukraine, and what has been the nature of local, national and external actors' involvement in it? These are the questions that the authors examine in this comprehensive analysis of the situation in Ukraine.

The crisis evolved from peaceful protests to full-scale military conflict and to an unstable ceasefire frequently interrupted by, at times, intense clashes between government forces and separatist rebels. Tracing the emergence of two new de-facto state entities in the post-Soviet space – the self-declared Donetsk and Luhansk people's republics – from the chaos of the early days after Russia's annexation of Crimea in Spring 2014 to the second Minsk Agreement in February 2015, and focusing on the actions of the immediate conflict parties and their external backers, the authors investigate the feasibility and viability of several prominent scenarios for a possible future settlement of the conflict.

As an in-depth case study of the complex dynamics of the conflict at local, national, regional and global levels of analysis, the book complements and advances existing scholarship on civil war and international crisis management, and also provides insights for the policy community and the wider interested public.

Tetyana Malyarenko is Professor of International Security and Jean Monnet Professor of European Security at the National University 'Odessa Law Academy,' Ukraine. She is the founder and director of the Ukrainian Institute for Crisis Management and Conflict Resolution, and has held visiting positions at Johns Hopkins University; the Wilson Centre for International Scholars; the University of California, Berkeley; the University of Granada; the University of Tromso; and the University of Gothenburg. An expert on post-conflict and post-authoritarian transitions, she is the author of numerous books, book chapters and journal articles in Ukrainian, English and Russian. Malyarenko earned her Masters, Candidate of Science, and Doctor of Science degrees from Donetsk State University of Management.

Stefan Wolff is Professor of International Security at the University of Birmingham, UK, and an Associate Fellow at the Royal United Services Institute in London. An expert on international crisis management and post-conflict state-building, he has published over 80 journal articles and book chapters, as well as 17 books, including *Ethnic Conflict: A Global Perspective* (Oxford University Press, 2007), *Conflict Management in Divided Societies: Theories and Practice* (Routledge, 2011, with Christalla Yakinthou) and *The European Union as a Conflict Manager* (Routledge, 2012, with Richard G. Whitman). Bridging the gap between academia and policy making, he frequently advises governments and international organisations and has been involved in various stages of peace negotiations, including in Africa, the Middle East and the post-Soviet space. Wolff graduated from the University of Leipzig, and holds an M.Phil. from the University of Cambridge and a Ph.D. from the London School of Economics and Political Science.

The Dynamics of Emerging De-Facto States

Eastern Ukraine in the Post-Soviet Space

Tetyana Malyarenko and Stefan Wolff

Routledge
Taylor & Francis Group

LONDON AND NEW YORK

First published 2019 by Routledge

2 Park Square, Milton Park, Abingdon, Oxfordshire OX14 4RN

52 Vanderbilt Avenue, New York, NY 10017

Routledge is an imprint of the Taylor & Francis Group, an informa business

First issued in paperback 2021

British Library Cataloguing-in-Publication Data
A catalogue record for this book is available from the British Library

Library of Congress Cataloging-in-Publication Data
A catalog record for this book has been requested

ISBN: 978-1-138-32884-6 (hbk)
ISBN: 978-1-03-209407-6 (pbk)
ISBN: 978-0-429-44840-9 (ebk)

Typeset in Times New Roman
by Apex CoVantage, LLC

Contents

Acknowledgements

This book is the result of several years of research and has benefitted from the support of many individuals and organisations.

Thanks are due to the NATO Defence College Rome (Partnership for Peace Programme), the Austrian Marshall Plan Foundation, and the Gerda Henkel Stiftung ("Strengthening Democratic Security Governance and the Rule of Law in Donbas: Civil-Military Cooperation and the Management of Current and Future Threats in Conflict-Affected Territories of Ukraine") for their support of Tetyana Malyarenko's work.

Stefan Wolff's research for this paper has been supported by a grant from the UK's Economic and Social Research Council (Research Grant ES/M009211/1: "Understanding and Managing Intra-State Territorial Contestation") and through funding from the University of Birmingham's ESRC Impact Acceleration Account.

Both authors have jointly received support from the NATO Science for Peace and Security Programme ("Enhancing Strategic Analytical Capabilities in NATO Partner Countries") and the EU's Jean Monnet Programme (Project Grant 2016-574646: "The EU's Comprehensive Approach to External Conflict and Crisis Management"). Some of the initial research was funded by the Centre for East European and International Studies, and we gratefully acknowledge the support of its Director, Professor Gwendolyn Sasse, who also shared with us her own insights into the situation in Ukraine.

We are also indebted to numerous colleagues who have provided invaluable feedback on earlier drafts of individual chapters, including members of NATO Defence College Senior Course 126, as well as Derek Averre, R. William Ayres, Argyro Kartsonaki, Nino Kemoklidze, George Kyris, Harris Mylonas, Kevork Oskanian, Thomas Funch Pedersen, Jasper de Quincey Adams, Olivier Schmitt, Gareth Stansfield, Mark Webber, and Kataryna Wolczuk.

The usual disclaimer remains.

Odesa and Birmingham,   Tetyana Malyarenko
November 2018   Stefan Wolff

1   Introduction

The conflict in Ukraine has evolved since 2013 from initially peaceful protests against then Ukrainian President Viktor Yanukovych's decision to delay the signature of an Association Agreement with the European Union (EU) to full-scale military conflict in 2014–2015 and to an unstable ceasefire interrupted by, at times, intense clashes between Ukrainian armed forces and separatist rebels in the Donbas region in the east of the country.

The conflict has had profound consequences locally, nationally and beyond Ukraine. Apart from the loss of life and physical destruction, it has caused the internal and external displacement of over two million people. The conflict has also led to the establishment of yet another de-facto entity (or, in fact, two) in the post-Soviet space, and one that dwarfs existing entities in geographical and population size. Due to the intense internationalisation of the conflict, the crisis in Ukraine has also been one of the most important drivers for the deterioration of relations between Russia and the West. As such, it poses one of the most critical contemporary challenges to European and international security.

Our aim in this book is to investigate the causes and consequences of the conflict in eastern Ukraine, and the responses to it so far by local, national and external actors. On this basis, we then examine the feasibility and viability of a number of options for the settlement of the conflict. In order to do so, we proceed as follows. We begin with a review of the existing literature on the conflict to date, identify some critical gaps and offer an overview of our own approach to understanding the dynamics of the emergence of the Donetsk and Luhansk people's republics (hereafter DPR and LPR), and what this reveals about the constraints and opportunities of conflict settlement. We then reflect on our methodology, discussing our data requirements and methods of data collection and analysis, considering in particular the ethical and other challenges of doing research in, and on, an ongoing low-intensity conflict. Turning to the empirical part of the book, we offer an analytical narrative of the emergence of the two de-facto entities in eastern

Ukraine, focusing on its causes and consequences, as well as the responses by various direct and indirect parties to the conflict, and demonstrating the connections between developments at local, national and regional/global levels of analysis. In a final section of the book, we then use this analysis to examine the feasibility and viability of several prominent scenarios identified in the existing academic and policy literature on a possible settlement of the conflict. We conclude with a summary of our argument and main findings, and highlight future research needs.

2   A blended conflict in an antagonistically penetrated region

A framework for understanding the conflict in eastern Ukraine

The existing debate on the conflict in eastern Ukraine

The body of existing literature on the conflict in eastern Ukraine has four defining characteristics:

1   A significant focus on geopolitical explanations and implications that sees 'great power' competition between Russia and the West (predominantly the EU, with some lesser focus on the North Atlantic Treaty Organization [NATO] and the US) as the major driver of conflict in eastern Ukraine.
2   Considerably less emphasis on domestic developments in Ukraine prior to, and since, the beginning of the crisis.
3   Some comparative work within each of these two major themes that is focused on the post-Soviet space and comparable situations, particularly in Moldova (Transnistria) and Georgia (Abkhazia and South Ossetia).
4   To the extent that existing research considers mitigation measures, these, too, are primarily examined in the context of Russia-West relations, rather than exploring the domestic level of analysis in Ukraine.

We consider each of these characteristics in turn now, and elaborate on the potential contribution each can make to a better understanding of the dynamics of the conflict to date and of the constraints and opportunities for its mitigation.

Geopolitical drivers of the conflict in eastern Ukraine

From early on in the evolution of the conflict in eastern Ukraine, geopolitical explanations have dominated the search for its causes. Initially also linked to the annexation of Crimea, the geopolitical interpretation of the conflict, often in combination with an examination of Russia's strategy of 'hybrid warfare,' has been remarkably stable over time and has not experienced many significant challenges. However, within this paradigm, there are important differences between key authors.

The geopolitical explanation of the origins and evolution of the conflict in eastern Ukraine takes several forms. On one side of the geopolitical continuum of explanations, Western ineptitude is considered from one perspective as the main trigger for the escalation of the crisis in late 2013 and early 2014, while on the opposite end, it is Russian expansionism. This division of opinion is particularly obvious in the US debate (McFaul, Sestanovich, and Sestanovich 2014; Mearsheimer 2014), but has also gained some traction in Europe (MacFarlane and Menon 2014). Unsurprisingly, Russian scholars and analysts find themselves in agreement with the view that Western actions, in their cumulative results since the early 1990s, have been the main driving force of the conflict in eastern Ukraine (Deliagin et al. 2015; Lukin 2014).

The middle ground between these two opposite ends of the geopolitical debate is occupied by views that argue that, regardless of whose actions (and/or perceptions) triggered the conflict, and somewhat independent now also of the wider crisis of Russia-West relations of which it is now but one manifestation, the conflict in eastern Ukraine quickly gained a dynamic of its own, fuelled to a significant degree by the actions of the external backers of domestic rivals (Cadier 2014; Charap 2014a, 2014b; Charap and Darden 2014; Dunn and Bobick 2014).

These and other similar views (Auer 2015; Götz 2015; Haukkala 2015; Kroenig 2015; Nováky 2015; Sakwa 2008; Smith 2015; Wolff 2015) focus predominantly on the geopolitical causes and consequences of the conflict in eastern Ukraine. Another, albeit much smaller, body of literature considers specifically military and military-strategic implications, including the highly contested notion of hybrid warfare (Allison 2014; Freedman 2014; Norberg and Westerlund 2014) and the impact of the conflict on the global nuclear order (Fitzpatrick 2014; Rublee 2015; Yost 2015).

While still largely situated in the geopolitical discussion of the conflict in eastern Ukraine, a number of authors consider somewhat different drivers of its evolution, including Russian consideration of its post-Soviet allies (Redman 2014; Vieira 2016) and the (soft-power) notion of the Russian world (Feklyunina 2015) and its opposing Ukrainian national identity projects (Kiryukhin 2016; Kulyk 2016; Marples 2016).

Finally, there is a small literature that engages more critically with geopolitical perspectives and seeks to integrate them into a more multi-faceted explanation of the crisis by either considering it broadly from the viewpoint of an evolving Russian identity (Hopf 2016) or emphasising the interaction between local/domestic and geopolitical factors (Schneckener 2016; Wilson 2016).

While not without its shortcomings, geopolitical interpretations of the conflict in eastern Ukraine are, in our view, critical to the understanding of the broader dynamics of its evolution over time and the possibilities of effective conflict mitigation. Regardless of whether one prioritises external (geopolitical) or domestic factors in conflict processes, policy makers need to carefully weigh both as they consider the impact of their approaches to the conflict in eastern Ukraine on these factors, and vice versa. Put differently, the value of geopolitical perspectives is that they represent one critical element not only of the drivers of the conflict but also of its management (and eventual settlement).

Domestic developments in Ukraine

A significantly smaller body of literature considers the domestic causes and consequences of the conflict in eastern Ukraine. Here we find accounts focused on (incompatible) identities (Cybriwsky 2014; Feklyunina 2015; Ishchenko 2016; Kulyk 2016; Matveeva 2016; Sotiriou 2016), institutional fragility (Fedorenko, Rybiy, and Umland 2016; Cleary 2016; Konończuk 2016; Molchanov 2016) and a flawed management of the initially negotiated transition (Hopf 2016; Robinson 2016; Schneckener 2016; Strasheim 2016).

Beyond that, there is a small, but empirically valuable, thread in the literature that considers individual motivations especially among paramilitary fighters on both sides of the conflict (Karagiannis 2016; Loshkariov and Sushentsov 2016; Malyarenko and Galbreath 2016; Matveeva 2016), while also highlighting the (initial) fluidity and contingency of societal cleavages (Onuch and Sasse 2016).

Taken together, these different perspectives on the domestic dimensions of the conflict in eastern Ukraine complement, rather than contradict, the geopolitical interpretations of the conflict. They offer a counterbalance to a view that conceives the conflict solely as a manifestation of a (re-)emerging geopolitical rivalry. Proper integration of both approaches would be an important prerequisite for a more focused analysis of settlement options for the conflict. The lack of the former, thus, in part, explains the absence of the latter.

Comparative perspectives

Relatively few sources take an explicit comparative perspective – and if they do, two such perspectives predominate: a view that takes the conflict in eastern Ukraine as another example of the emergence of de-facto (or unrecognised) states (Gardner 2016; German 2016; Istomin and Bolgova

2016; Kemp 2014; Kennedy 2016) and a view that compares and contrasts the approaches taken by Russia and the West (primarily, the EU) in relation to the conflict in eastern Ukraine or the contested neighbourhood of the post-Soviet space more broadly (Cadier 2014; Nilsson and Silander 2016; Nitoiu 2016), including the promotion of competing regime types (Bunce and Hozic 2015; Smith 2015; Tolstrup 2015).

The value of such comparative perspectives is twofold. On the one hand, they allow us to consider the conflict in eastern Ukraine in the context of a broader type of cases of de-facto (or unrecognised) states. As several of these have existed for decades within and beyond the post-Soviet space, comparative insights can assist in developing sustainable strategies for mitigating the (human) security risks associated with these conflicts and for more effectively containing the inevitable negative consequences of often ill-conceived conflict management strategies (Gerrits and Bader 2016; Hughes and Sasse 2016; Sasse 2009).

On the other hand, and closely associated with this latter point, understanding the consequences of rival external involvement in situations of emerging and consolidating de-facto entities can lead to the development of better conflict mitigation strategies that foresee, and ideally avoid, the negative local fallout of geopolitical competition (Beyer and Wolff 2016).

Mitigation measures

There is relatively little substantive analysis of actual mitigation measures that could be applied to managing the situation in eastern Ukraine. Some literature exists that considers, and focuses on, de-escalation of the crisis between Russia and the West (Charap 2014a; Charap and Darden 2014; Freedman 2014; Legvold 2014; Yurgens 2015). In addition, between 2016 and early 2018, several proposals were made for the deployment of United Nations (UN) peacekeepers to Donbas by both Western (International Crisis Group 2017, 2018; Melnyk and Umland 2016; Umland 2018; Vershbow 2018) and Russian (Kortunbov 2017) commentators and analysts, yet since the publication of a detailed report (Gowan 2018) to this effect by the Hudson Institute in Washington, this debate has largely subsided. While peacekeeping may play a facilitating role in conflict management and potentially, conflict settlement through the establishment of conditions under which a settlement concerning eastern Ukraine's status within Ukraine could be negotiated, implemented and sustained, there is very little analysis of the substance of a feasible and viable settlement. Among the few existing publications that consider this dimension of the conflict, Strasheim (2016) implicitly argues for the need for properly guaranteed power sharing institutions.

Moving beyond existing debates: from understanding the dynamics of the origins and evolution of the DPR and LPR to a settlement of the conflict

As indicated previously, an examination of the existing body of literature on the conflict in eastern Ukraine leads us to two main conclusions. The first is that scholarship and analysis in relation to the conflict in eastern Ukraine so far has interpreted its causes and consequences primarily through a geopolitical lens and focused on its external dynamics. Even when domestic factors are considered, existing research to date, with few exceptions, lacks serious efforts to integrate both perspectives. Second, and partially as a consequence of the first, research on conflict mitigation in eastern Ukraine is very sparse, especially when it comes to thinking about comprehensive models for achieving a viable Ukrainian state within the current context of geopolitical competition between the main external protagonists in the conflict.

Consequently, we find a significant gap in current research endeavours concerning a sustainable settlement of the conflict in eastern Ukraine. Filling this gap will require a more sustained effort at synthesising existing research on the domestic and external drivers of the conflict, and integrating it with research on feasible and viable settlements of intra-state territorial disputes in the context of emerging and consolidating de-facto entities. In order to do this, however, we must first reflect on the nature of the conflict in eastern Ukraine and its theoretical implications.

The conflict in Ukraine is part of a longer 'tradition' of similar conflicts in Eastern Europe that date back to the late 1980s. In the context of Soviet institutions' decreasing capacity and willingness to manage the multiple challenges of managing a highly complex and diverse state, conflicts that had previously been simmering below the surface became more obvious both within and between the former Soviet republics and across a range of formal and informal structures. As the Soviet Union eventually disintegrated in 1991, further conflicts erupted, laying bare changing power relations and the way they played out between self-asserting and re-asserting, often reciprocally contested and increasingly non-inclusive, identities that frequently formed the basis for mobilising groups into conflict with each other. This resurgence of 'identity conflicts' was not a purely post-Soviet phenomenon: the former Yugoslavia and the former communist countries in East-Central Europe experienced similar challenges, albeit of different scale and intensity.

Notwithstanding significant differences in the setting and dynamics of these various conflicts, they all occurred in a context of transitional openings when agents of change had brief but promising opportunities to reconfigure their states' underpinning institutional structures. The decisions taken at these critical junctures gave rise to contested, and thus far in many cases incomplete, processes of state-building and nation-building (Csergő, Roseberry, and Wolff 2017). Yet, the dynamics of conflicts emerging in this period 25–30 years ago did not only have local-level and state-level consequences, but increasingly intersected with regional-level and global-level developments. As a consequence, we argue, the protracted conflicts over Abkhazia, South Ossetia, Transnistria and the Nagorno-Karabakh territory, and the more recent crisis in Ukraine, constitute blended conflicts that play out in an antagonistically penetrated region.

How do we conceptualise, and subsequently operationalise, 'blended conflict' and 'penetrated region'? In our view, 'blended' is more than multi-layered, multi-faceted, and multi-dimensional, as well as more than multi-level; it is about the dynamic connectedness of actors, structures and other factors at and across different levels of analysis: horizontally, vertically and 'diagonally.'

The notion of 'blended,' thus, already implies a degree of 'penetration'; that is, a significant role for actors that are external to the state and/or the region in which the conflict is situated or where it originated. Penetration adds to conflict complexity, especially when the penetrating outsiders are, or grow to become, antagonists. As is the case with conflicts in the post-Soviet space, local conflicts then become overlaid with external antagonisms and easily turn into another arena of regional-level and/or global-level rivalries. This is not to say that they do not retain a dynamic of their own, but this 'Eigendynamik' (or momentum) ebbs and flows very much in relation to the intensity of 'active' penetration. Thus, multiple actors and alliances of actors on the ground and beyond are in constant flux and contextually variable, not least because their agendas differ from local to global aspirations with punctual but not sustainable overlap. Geopolitical aspirations of regional and great powers, domestic elites operating in a context of often fragile states with weak institutions that are unable to provide security and other basic public goods, local and trans-national organised criminal networks, and local actors with legitimate grievances couched in the language of human rights and self-determination have a tendency to create a toxic and contagious brew of challenges that are difficult to manage domestically, regionally and globally.

As a consequence, blended conflicts in antagonistically penetrated regions are also characterised by intense internationalisation. External actors with opportunistic and strategic motivations are more easily drawn into conflicts, are more willing to exploit and stoke local tensions, and are more adept at bargaining locally, regionally and globally over their involvement in conflicts. Such external actors have different relationships with each other over different issues across different arenas of interaction: the West

(EU/NATO/US) and Russia have interacted very differently over Ukraine, Syria, North Korea and Iran, as well as over terrorism, organised crime, climate change, etc. Blended conflicts in antagonistically penetrated regions are, thus, also a new manifestation of multi-polarity, in the sense of not only multiple centres of power, but also multiple arenas in which these centres of power pursue different interests in different, and constantly evolving, alliance configurations.

At the same time, external actors also have different relationships with the local actors they support or constrain. Such variation exists in the level of control they exercise, the 'due diligence' they conduct before committing or withdrawing support and the resulting proliferation of more local actors soliciting external support. Different external-local relationships also manifest themselves in the ways in which forms and means of external support vary: from direct military, material, technical and financial supply lines to political and diplomatic backing of presumptive allies, be they incumbent governments or their challengers. On top of that, forms and means of external support also interact in more complex ways: overt and covert forms of support and their gradual or abrupt increase or (dis-)continuation have unintended and unforeseen consequences that shape conflict trajectories and constrain or enable conflict settlement opportunities.

We need, thus, an approach towards blended conflicts in penetrated regions that is able to integrate different theoretical frameworks in order to be able to explain the causes of such conflicts, the factors that facilitated their continuation, and the conditions for their sustainable settlement. Such an approach, naturally, needs to begin with identifying relevant theories of conflict and conflict settlement.

A significant number of studies have shown the impact of identity-related factors in the outbreak of conflict. Such theories claim identity issues as the main underlying cause of a given conflict, but also acknowledge that identity is rarely its sole cause. Hence, scholars have attempted to discover what the reasons are that alongside identity-related grievances motivate and enable the outbreak of violent conflict. Theuerkauf (2010a), for instance, stresses the effects of political exclusion on the outbreak of conflict. Gurr (1993) and Gurr and Moore (1997) also focus on political grievances and grievances related to status loss as main motivator of conflict, a view also shared by Cederman, Wimmer, and Min (2010) and Siroky and Cuffe (2014). As we demonstrate further ahead, identity was a significant driver of the conflict in eastern Ukraine, but it became relevant precisely in the context of increasing political exclusion which eroded a previously relatively sustainable framework in which local, regional and national identities managed to co-exist rather than challenge an overall social, political and legal consensus on Ukrainian statehood.

As noted in existing literature on the causes of conflict and clearly applicable to the situation in Ukraine, political exclusion and weak state structures and a lack of democratic culture tend to mutually reinforce each other as a main cause of intra-state conflict (Mengisteab 2003; Posen 1993; Rwantabagu 2001). Theuerkauf (2010b), Posen (1993) and van Evera (1994) suggest that political exclusion and weak state structures lead to a security dilemma, which increases the likelihood of conflict. The security dilemma is one of the most commonly accepted causal mechanisms that links grievances to conflict onset (Horowitz 1985; Kaufman 2001; Kaufmann 1996; Lake and Rothchild 1996; Rose 2000), making mutual distrust between groups one of the most problematic psychological elements of any conflict situation (Fearon and Laitin 2008). Such distrust now permeates each and every of the partially overlapping conflicts in Ukraine that constitute its blended nature and, as we demonstrate further ahead, inhibit its settlement and in fact make renewed escalation a distinct possibility.

However important and relevant as it is, political exclusion is not the only factor that may escalate identity grievances to violent conflict. Economic grievances and poverty (Collier and Hoeffler 1998; Fearon and Laitin 2003), as well as corruption (Neudorfer and Theuerkauf 2014), have been found to be equally important reasons, and their relevance in Ukraine is beyond question. What is more, as Stewart (2010) has demonstrated, violent mobilisation is more likely when a group that shares a distinct identity faces severe inequalities in economic, social, political or cultural terms. Since her ground-breaking findings, this notion of horizontal inequalities as primary motivation for conflict have been used in numerous studies especially in sub-Saharan Africa (Diprose and Ukiwo 2008; Langer 2015; Marc et al. 2013; Østby, Nordås, and Rød 2009) and South Asia (Diprose 2009; Murshed and Gates 2005; Østby et al. 2011; Parks, Colletta, and Oppenheim 2013), while some scholars focused in specific on the role of regional inequalities to the onset of secessionist conflicts (Bakke and Wibbels 2006; Buhaug and Rød 2006; Deiwiks, Cederman, and Gleditsch 2012). Ukraine has clearly been affected by such regional horizontal inequalities. While Donbas was historically among the wealthier regions of the country, it was the very threat to this wealth, perceived by both the political-economic elites and citizens in the wake of the Euromaidan civil unrest that proved a critical catalyst towards conflict escalation. As we further illustrate ahead, the conflict in Donbas, thus, also attests to another now well-established finding in the literature on conflict causes: namely, that larger groups find it easier to mobilise for collective action, provided the presence of powerful motivations (see, for example, Cederman, Buhaug, and Rød 2009).

Other scholars, however, reject the notion that identity constitutes the primary cause of conflict, while focusing more on how elites use power vacuums, weak institutions and economic decline in order to 'ethnicise' territory and fuel violence by creating perceptions of identity that did not exist before (Gagnon 2004). While we do not find evidence in the case of Ukraine that the conflict's identity dynamics were created out of thin air, the power vacuum that emerged following the Euromaidan events in Kyiv and the general chaos subsequently ensuing in Donbas, the Ukrainian state's fragile institutions and the perceived threat of imminent economic decline as a direct consequence of changing power dynamics locally and at the centre clearly contributed to the escalation of violent conflict in Donbas.

Geography has also been widely researched as a factor enabling conflict, examining how access (Collier and Hoeffler 2005) and/or competition over lootable (Humphreys 2005; Lujala, Gleditsch, and Gilmore 2005) and non-lootable (Collier and Hoeffler 2004; Fearon 2005) resources, food and water (Wischnath and Buhaug 2014) may lead to violent conflict. As we further explore ahead, competition over resources – especially in the form of assets that became 'available' in the wake of the ouster of President Yanukovych – was a significant dimension not only in the local conflicts between different criminal networks in the early phases of the conflict in eastern Ukraine but also continuing into the present, as evident in long-running turf wars between different criminal gangs in the self-declared republics and their ties with political and economic elites there, as well as in Ukraine and Russia.

Buhaug (2006), Buhaug, Gates, and Lujala (2009) and Weidmann (2009) have also studied geography in terms of location, i.e., how, among other things, the absolute and relative distance from the capital and the proximity to international borders affect the outbreak of conflict. That this is relevant in the Ukrainian crisis can hardly be disputed, and is particularly the location of Donbas in eastern Ukraine and on the border with Russia that has had, and continues to have, a significant effect on the conflict. This particular geography of the conflict is relevant in terms of the region's history and identity, the ease with which Russia could support its local proxies and the difficulties that the government in Kyiv faced in asserting its authority beyond the capital. Moreover, Russia's annexation of Crimea and the construction of a bridge linking Russia with Crimea across the Kerch Strait has further increased the strategic significance of both rebel-controlled and government-controlled territories in eastern Ukraine, increasing the risk of further conflict escalation.

Ukraine is thus an obvious example of the well-established facts that contemporary intra-state conflict is rarely limited within the borders of a single state, and that the factors that determine its onset, duration, intensity and termination are not to be found only within its territory. Therefore, a considerable number of scholars have examined how external interventions may influence the outbreak of an internal conflict. For example, Oberschall

(2000) and Glaurdić (2016), discussing the Yugoslav wars, have demonstrated how the end of the Cold War had an effect on the outbreak of conflict, while Ayoob (1999) and Ehteshami and Elik (2011) have pointed out that global developments affect foreign policy and security both in the Middle East in particular and in other highly penetrated regions in general. Alongside global factors, the role of neighbourhood has also been widely researched (Brown 2001; Kubo 2010; Salehyan 2007; Sambanis 2001). Political activists in one country can obtain support from transnational kin groups, affecting the balance of power within that country (Cederman, Girardin, and Gleditsch 2009; Salehyan 2007), while refugees, ethnic leaders seeking sanctuary in another state, and partisan interventions on behalf of such groups, as well as international diplomatic activity, also contribute to the internationalisation of conflict (Bercovitch 2003). Clearly, the crisis in Ukraine that we focus on here is one of these cases of an extensively internationalised conflict. Yet, as we demonstrate in our analysis, the quality of its internationalisation is rather distinct. In line with our notion of a blended conflict in an antagonistically penetrated region, what we face here is in fact a multitude of partially overlapping conflicts in which different domestic and external conflict parties have equally distinct and yet interrelated and often conflicting relationships with each other that have an impact on the dynamics of the 'original' conflict, as well as on the prospects of any sustainable solution of either individual of these conflicts or the blended conflict as a whole.

What is particularly striking in the case of the crisis in Ukraine are the links between local-level, regional-level and global-level dynamics. The regional level is of specific significance here, as it connects local dynamics in eastern Ukraine 'horizontally' to the complexities of other similar conflicts in Georgia and Moldova, while linking them 'vertically' to the game of competitive influence-seeking in which Russia and the West are locked in the contested neighbourhood of the post-Soviet space (Malyarenko and Wolff 2018). This importance of the region as a distinct level of analysis has been thoroughly examined by Buzan and Waever (2003) in their work developing the regional security complex theory, as well as by Kelly (2007) and Wolff (2011b). The latter focuses on the regional dimensions of state failure, and thus provides another empirical and conceptual link across different levels of analysis that is relevant in the case of Ukraine – the catalytic effects of fragile domestic institutions in the genesis and evolution of blended conflicts (see also Beyer and Wolff 2016).

As previously indicated, in order to be able to integrate these different approaches into our single analytical framework based on the concept of a blended conflict, we adopt a levels of analysis approach in our book that considers the main causes and consequences of the conflict in eastern

Ukraine, as well as the responses by relevant domestic and external actors, at three levels of analysis – the local (i.e., in the rebel-controlled and Ukrainian-controlled areas of the Donetsk and Luhansk regions), the national (i.e., Ukraine) and the regional/global (the post-Soviet space as the shared neighbourhood contested between the West and Russia). In doing so, we follow Cordell and Wolff (2009, 21), who emphasise that:

> [A]nalogous to understanding the causes of ethnic conflict as located in the complex interplay of different factors at local, state, regional and global levels of analysis, we must contextualise the success or failure of conflict settlement in the same way in order to explain why some policies work and others fail.

We also follow Wolff (2011a, 176), who wrote "that the success of conflict management depends on the dynamic relationship between the content of an agreement on institutional structures and the context within which it is achieved," i.e., a settlement needs to be feasible in the sense that it can be adopted by the conflict parties in the course of their negotiations, and it needs to be viable in the sense that it offers a functional institutional compromise that allows them to manage their differences in non-violent ways.

The crisis in Ukraine: applying the blended conflict lens

These different perspectives on conflict and conflict management can further help us to make sense of the crisis in Ukraine as we apply our blended conflict lens to this particular situation and its various dynamics, in particular when we consider that what is commonly referred to as 'the Ukraine crisis' consists of several distinct but closely related and partially overlapping conflicts. This is not only true for the distinction between the conflict concerning Crimea (which we do not cover in our analysis) and that in Donbas, but also regarding the latter taken on its own. We can thus distinguish from among six different dimensions of conflict that reflect both different dynamics of origin and evolution and different sets of actors with often incompatible agendas concerning the management and possible settlement of the blended conflict as a whole or of individual dimensions within it:

1   The 'original' Maidan conflict. Triggered by President Yanukovych's refusal to sign the Association Agreement with the EU as planned at the Eastern Partnership Summit in Vilnius, Lithuania, pro-European protests in Kyiv's Independence Square quickly gained traction and expanded over the course of December 2013 and January 2014. As the confrontation between protesters and security forces grew increasingly

violent, negotiations between Yanukovych and the parliamentary opposition were mediated by the German, French and Polish foreign ministers in the presence of a senior Russian diplomat and resulted in the Kyiv agreement of February 2014, which provided for a transition period until the end of 2014, including a government of national unity comprising representatives of all main parliamentary parties, a process of constitutional reform aimed at re-balancing the powers of parliament and president, and, following the completion of the constitutional reform process, presidential elections. Rejected as insufficient by the protesters on the Maidan, the agreement collapsed within days and President Yanukovych was forced into exile in Russia. This series of events then gave rise to a proliferation of conflict across five additional dimensions (Workshops E, J, L, M).

2   An (elite-driven) conflict between local elites in Donbas ('Donetskiye') and the government in Kyiv over demands for greater local self-government. Facing the prospect of political marginalisation at the centre after the departure of President Yanukovych, established local elites that had served as Yanukovych's power base were keen to maximise their local autonomy in order to protect their local assets and thrive economically (Interviews 5, 6; Workshops I, J).

3   A second (elite-driven) conflict between different of local elites in Ukraine (primarily 'Donetskiye' versus 'Dnipropetrovskiye') and between different factions within the group of 'Donetskiye.' Following the sudden departure of Yanukovych, considerable assets and income sources previously under the control of the president and his clan gave rise to significant turf wars among different constellations of local elites and their networks in politics, business and organised crime. In addition, Ukrainian oligarch Igor Kolomoysky, through his subordinate Gennady Korban, established and funded a number of anti-rebel paramilitary battalions (including 'Dnepr,' 'Azov' and 'Donbas') which he used as his private armies in pursuit of wresting control over strategic assets from Donetsk oligarchs, primarily Rinat Akhmetov's and Dmitry Firtash's holdings in the energy sector. A subsequent conflict between Kolomoysky and President Petro Poroshenko quickly put an end to these ambitions and led to Kolomoysky's emigration (Interview 9, 10; Workshops A, G).

4   A (mass-driven) conflict, the so-called anti-Maidan, between a more pro-Russia population in eastern Ukraine and the newly formed government in Kyiv. Initially, non-violent protests were organized by leaders of local communities; these protests were motivated by fears and resentment of a new government in Kyiv that lacked legitimacy in the eyes of local protesters. However, this protest movement lacked

meaningful and effective coordination from the beginning, and after the flight of the local Ukrainian elite from Donbas, it rapidly fragmented and degenerated into warlordism (Interview 10; Workshops B, D, F).

5   Antagonistic penetration of these more localised conflicts, related to the final two dimensions of the blended conflict in Ukraine. On the one hand, there is the Russia-driven and supported effort aimed at the destabilization of the pro-Western government in Kyiv that has been at the heart of the violent conflict in Donbas since 2014 and accounts for the overwhelming majority of conflict-related deaths, displacement and destruction. Frequently considered a hybrid or proxy war, this dimension of the conflict is best described as an internationalised intra-state conflict. Interviews 12, 13, 18. Workshops G, K, L.

6   Much briefer in duration and far less violent, the annexation of Crimea by Russia in the spring of 2014 constitutes the other aspect of antagonistic penetration in the Ukraine crisis. While clearly having a local dimension as well, this is much more of an inter-state conflict between Russia and Ukraine. Moreover, it constitutes a major violation of the spirit and the letter of the 1975 Helsinki Final Act and the nascent collaborative security order in Europe that had subsequently been built on it. Yet, the annexation of Crimea was not the first violation in this regard. Kosovo's contested secession from Serbia in February 2008 and Russia's recognition of the independence of Abkhazia and South Ossetia in August the same year are, arguably, precursors of the developments in Ukraine from late 2013 onwards, highlighting the geopolitical competition between Russia and the West as a major driver of Ukraine's blended conflict and illustrating its antagonistic penetration by rival great powers. Interviews 15, 18, 20. Workshops K, L.

Applying, as we just have, our blended conflict lens to the crisis in Ukraine enables us to identify the different simultaneous and partially overlapping conflicts in Ukraine since late 2013 and highlight the extent to which they are co-constitutive and the degree to which the different conflict parties act and interact at local, national and regional/global levels. Identifying and analysing the situation in Ukraine from this conflict-focused perspective allows us to pay sufficient attention to actors, structures and the context in which they operate. In this sense, the blended conflict lens requires us to distinguish and analyse different actors' agendas as a reflection of the complexity of their different motivations. As these agendas are being implemented, they necessarily come into conflict with each other and have to confront the different constraints and opportunities that arise in the context of historically grown social, political, economic and cultural structures. Our analysis of the crisis in Ukraine as a blended conflict and the dynamics of its evolution from peaceful protest to separatist civil war that it enables, in turn, provides the foundation upon which we can consider different scenarios of conflict settlement.

Plan of the book

As indicated in our review of the existing literature, the geopolitical aspect of the conflict in eastern Ukraine that is part and parcel of this final conflict dimension has been a major focus of analysis to date. Given its significance, this is neither surprising nor unwarranted. However, the conflict in eastern Ukraine is clearly more complex than such a narrow focus and this dimension of the conflict cannot be fully understood in isolation from other conflict dimensions. Put differently, despite the increasing quantity of literature on the conflict in eastern Ukraine, we still lack a comprehensive understanding of its drivers both in the sense of initial conflict causes and the dynamics they subsequently gave rise to that have now turned this conflict into yet another protracted post-Soviet conflict. This gap, in turn, also leads to an incomplete understanding of what settlements may be feasible and viable; that is, what institutions can the conflict parties and external stakeholders agree on, implement and operate such that a sustainable settlement of the conflict becomes possible.

Adopting the blended conflict perspective just outlined, our empirical analysis in the following focuses on three main themes. In Chapter 3, we first provide a background narrative to the origins and evolution of the crisis in Ukraine from late 2013 to the summer of 2014. This period of approximately seven months between November 2013 (Yanukovych's refusal to go ahead with signing the Association Agreement with the EU) and July 2014 (the beginning of concerted state-building efforts by Russia) is largely characterised by an array of distinct developments in Donbas, including several parallel conflicts there and within Ukraine as noted previously. While the Maidan conflict in Kyiv was 'resolved' following Yanukovych's flight to Russia in late February 2014, Russian involvement in the multiple conflicts in Donbas was limited, compared to developments after July 2014. During this period, Moscow's main focus was on Crimea, with the illegal annexation of the peninsula completed in late April 2014. While Russian involvement in Donbas increased thereafter, it still lacked the systematic state-building effort that becomes apparent from July 2014 onwards. This frames our subsequent discussion of the political, social and economic consequences of the conflict with a particular view on the local processes of identity transformation and state-building in the rebel-controlled territories and way these were shaped by, and in turn shaped, responses by the Ukrainian government, Russia and the West.

Second, we examine the evolution of identity in eastern Ukraine since the country's independence in 1991 to the beginning of the conflict and its subsequent, albeit as-yet-incomplete, transformation in Chapter 4. This is an important dimension of the conflict in two ways. On the one hand, it helps us to understand better the initial conflict dynamics in Donbas between late 2013 and summer 2014. On the other hand, it contributes to the understanding of subsequent developments locally in Donbas, nationally in Ukraine, and regionally with a view to Russian policies vis-à-vis Kyiv and Donbas. Put differently, the evolution of local identity prior to the beginning of the conflict and thereafter is a critical component in our argument related to the emergence of the de-facto entities in the DPR and LPR, and has a bearing on the feasibility and viability of various conflict settlement scenarios.

In Chapter 5, we consider the Russian-sponsored state-building efforts in the two de-facto entities from summer 2014 onwards. With the annexation of Crimea complete, anarchy in Donbas widespread and no progress being made with the implementation of the Geneva Declaration, Russia had both an opportunity and a need to extend and consolidate its control in Donbas. State-building from summer 2014 was accompanied by a significant increase in the intensity of fighting on the ground, first in late summer 2014 (prior to Minsk I), and then at the end of 2014 and again in early 2015 (leading to Minsk II). The de-facto states thus built have subsequently solidified their control of the territories they occupy in eastern Ukraine, even though they are far from stable entities – not only does the ceasefire remain highly volatile experiencing almost-daily violations on both sides, but the respective regimes in the DPR and LPR have been plagued by continuous infighting, evident most recently from the assassination of the DPR's 'head of state,' Alexander Zakharchenko.

The dynamics and outcomes of the parallel and closely intertwined processes of identity and state-building have a significant impact on the feasibility and viability of any conflict settlement, as we argue in Chapter 6. Building on the examination of conflict dynamics from the Kyiv Agreement in February 2014 to the second Minsk Agreement of February 2015 that we develop in our analytical narrative, we investigate what this tells us about the adoptability and functionality of three prominent scenarios currently being discussed – the so-called Croatian, Transnistrian and German scenarios. We briefly discuss the underlying assumptions of each scenario and the main opportunities and constraints for their realisation. By way of conclusion, we summarise in Chapter 7 our main argument and findings and highlight the need to be wary of accepting what may eventually prove an unsustainable new status quo.

Methodological considerations

Before embarking on our empirical analysis, it is important to reflect on our methodological approach, with a view of outlining its strengths and limitations. This is particularly important given the nature of our inquiry and the characteristics of the research environment in which we conducted it, as well as the potential policy implications of our findings. This very possibility of policy impact presents an obvious opportunity for social scientists, but it puts the challenges of research into even starker relief. *How* we know takes on a very different quality of both obligation and responsibility if *what* we know can shape the outcomes of peace negotiations, decisions to intervene militarily in foreign conflicts or policies to fund humanitarian relief efforts.

How we know and what we know is as much a theoretical and empirical issue as it is a methodological one. In the broad field of peace and conflict studies, case studies like ours often involve significant levels of fieldwork in a context that is not always conducive to this approach. Collecting data in and on a fragile and conflict-affected environment, in which a multitude of actors relate to each other in highly dynamic contexts, and on what often are politically highly sensitive and emotionally charged topics, poses significant challenges. These include that data is often relatively limited and its accuracy not always beyond doubt. Sources may be difficult to identify and to access, and their credibility is at times questionable. Moreover, even when interlocutors are willing to share information, they may be exposed to retribution, and researchers are also potentially at risk. As a consequence, data is often even more imperfect than usual; this has follow-on effects for both data analysis methods and the robustness of any inferences drawn, and, in turn, may limit the generalisability of any conclusions and the ability of researchers to offer credible policy recommendations.

Our project is above all an "intensive study of a single case" (Gerring 2007, Kindle location 208). We are interested in understanding one particular outcome – the emergence of de-facto entities in Donbas – in a specific instance – during the crisis in Ukraine, specifically between late 2013 and mid-2015. Case studies are variously described as thick narratives, thick descriptions or analytical narratives that enable researchers to develop "a more complete story with actors, motives, stages, and causal mechanisms that move the plot along" (Coppedge 2012, Kindle locations 3368–3370). This enables us to focus on the causal mechanism or pathway and "to locate the intermediate factors lying between some structural cause and its purported effect" (Gerring 2007, Kindle location 521–522). Note, however, that our approach is more akin to a causes-of-effects approach (Gerring 2012, 332ff.), trying to elucidate comprehensively what caused the emergence of the two de-facto entities in eastern Ukraine. While we cannot with certainty claim that we succeed in doing this (i.e., identify all causes and combinations of causes accounting for the observed outcome), our inquiry is designed in such a way that it is at least likely to achieve this, including through its embeddedness in the analytical framework of blended conflict and the combination of particular methods of data collection and analysis that we detail ahead.

When we began this project in February 2014, Ukraine was experiencing an acute crisis which led to the ouster of its then president and the formation of a new government, and which also triggered a number of turf wars among oligarchs. This was followed by two severe external challenges to the country's sovereignty and territorial integrity: the Russian annexation of Crimea and a Russian-supported separatist insurgency in Donbas, the latter of which quickly evolved into an intensely violent conflict costing approximately ten thousand lives, displacing over two million people, and causing significant physical destruction and economic disruption. By the time of writing (summer 2018), the conflict still simmers and occasionally flares up at a ceasefire line established in February 2015 that separates government-controlled and rebel-controlled territories. Doing research in such a volatile environment poses several challenges.

First, we needed to consider our data requirements and, based on that, issues of data collection. Our framework of understanding the emergence of the de-facto entities in Donbas as underpinned by the dynamics of a blended conflict in an antagonistically penetrated region provides sufficient guidance on data requirements, even though our research is not primarily deductive in nature. While the generation of our core concepts – blended conflict and penetrated region – is primarily based on inductive observation, the more detailed examination of the conflict in Donbas is, at least to some extent, more deductive in that it uses these concepts for systematic and structured observation. Yet, as these two concepts are not yet integrated into a well-formed theory, we have no basis for deriving and testing hypotheses, and in this sense our case study of the conflict in Donbas is more of the hypothesis-generating kind. Nonetheless, the way we conceptualise blended conflicts in an antagonistically penetrated region is suggestive of the need to collect data at the local, regional and global levels of analysis that can help us trace the process of the emergence of the two de-facto entities in Donbas. Sources of such data are first of all key decision-makers at each of these levels, including local and central government officials and key power brokers in Ukraine, officials in relevant international organisations in their headquarters and based in the country. These data can be obtained through interviews, focus groups and participant observation, as well as through official statements and published third-party interviews. Additionally, academic experts and analysts who follow the same case can be useful sources of information (either through their published work or through interviews and focus groups), as well as a sounding board for ideas that develop in the course of fieldwork and desk research. Official documents (such as the joint declarations and agreements concluded in the process of settlement negotiations) formed another source of data that we relied on, as did media coverage, primarily in Ukraine and Russia and originating from the two de-facto entities.

Over time, it became necessary for us to carefully reflect on, and adjust, our data-collection strategy. Our investigation of the dynamics underpinning the emergence of the two de-facto entities in Donbas started out as an empirical, curiosity-driven project that initially evolved opportunistically out of our interest in the events around the Maidan from November 2013 onwards. As the trajectory of developments in eastern Ukraine began to point more and more clearly into the direction of new de-facto entities being established, we began to follow this process more systematically, initially with a focus on the various rounds and formats of negotiations and the fate of the various agreements signed. At this stage, our empirical research consisted primarily of closely following events on the ground and in the media and interviewing key informants in local and central government in Ukraine, in Ukraine-based missions of international organisations and in their headquarters.

During the summer of 2014, conditions for fieldwork in eastern Ukraine, and particularly in Donbas, became more hazardous for both researcher and interlocutors, all but ruling out the continuation of key informant interviews in or near the conflict zone. Therefore, we began to rely more on internet-based media sources that by then had started to carry statements from, and interviews with, leading officials of the rebel governments. While we were not able to ask our own questions in those situations, the issues addressed in these broadcasts covered many areas of interest to us. Moreover, comparing such third-party interviews to those that we had been able to carry out before the deterioration in the security situation in Donbas, we found that they were generally no more or less credible than the ones we had conducted ourselves and thus constituted a reasonable adjustment to our data-collection strategy.

We faced a similar problem, albeit for different reasons, with our interviews with key informants from Russia. As we were unable to gain direct access to senior government sources, we relied on published statements, transcripts of news conferences and readouts from bilateral telephone conversations. We had better access to academic experts and analysts, partly through our established networks that predated the crisis in Ukraine. While participation of our Russian contacts in workshops we organised in Ukraine had become impossible from mid-2014 onwards, we were still able to conduct interviews with them via e-mail and Skype, or in third-country locations. Taken together, this allowed us to reconstruct in detail Russia's perception of the conflict and trace the evolution of its policies since late 2013.

We had no comparable problems concerning access to Ukrainian or international key informants (policy makers, analysts, academic experts) and were able to conduct a significant number of interviews over the course of several years, including with contacts in Ukraine, in the Organization for Security and Co-operation in Europe (OSCE), the EU, the United Nations Development Programme (UNDP) and the World Bank.

In total, we conducted sixty-five interviews between April 2014 and August 2018 and discussed our research in thirteen workshops in the same period of time. The latter, involving a range of participants from junior academics to seasoned analysts and senior government officials, was one of our strategies to corroborate data obtained from other sources and to sense-check our own analysis and interpretation of the wealth of information that we gradually built up.

While we used these workshops as an integrated part of our research strategy, they were not our only means of triangulation. We also tried to ensure as comprehensively as possible that we did not rely on just one data source or type of data source in supporting a particular claim by cross-checking information across interview transcripts and/or media reports and/or official documents. Where we conducted repeated interviews with the same source, we would return to issues raised in earlier interviews. We generally used later interviews in the data-collection process to discuss information obtained from a range of earlier sources. Where discrepancies became obvious, we used our best joint judgement to 'adjudicate' between sources; where we could not reach consensus, we did not rely on the piece of information concerned in our argument.

It is also worth noting that we were able to access original data in Ukrainian, Russian, English and German, and conduct interviews in all but a small handful of cases in the interlocutor's mother tongue.[1] This enabled us to pick up nuances and to establish good personal rapport with our informants.

This data-collection strategy thus produced a rich set of observations. At the same time, our pre-existing knowledge of Ukraine and the post-Soviet space more generally and our assumptions about blended conflicts in antagonistically penetrated regions form a "comprehensible universe of causal relations" (Gerring 2012, 331), in which we make a number of general assumptions about how the world 'works' in such a situation. Taken together, the nature of our data and our ability to interpret them in a structured way require, and enable, us to use causal-process observations to develop a thick analytical narrative of the developments leading to the emergence of the two de-facto entities in Donbas. In doing this, we specify a particular pathway through which this outcome developed. Partly because of the inductive nature of our approach (i.e., we did not have preconceived notions of how the outcome would emerge), and partly because of the real-time research that we conducted as events unfolded on the ground, we do not systematically consider alternative explanations. Rather, our goal is to use our analysis of the events that unfolded from late 2013 in and around Ukraine to establish a credible and well-substantiated causal pathway "that [is] consistent with the outcome and the process-tracing evidence" (George and Bennett 2005, 207) in this particular case.

Note

1 Exceptions included French native speakers in international organisations (interviews conducted in English) and the occasional native German speaker who preferred that the interview be conducted in English.

3 Origins and early developments of the conflict, November 2013– July 2014

After years of negotiations on an Association Agreement with the EU, the government of President Viktor Yanukovych suspended Ukraine's negotiations with Brussels on 21 November 2013, one week before a planned Eastern Partnership Summit in Vilnius where the Association Agreement was meant to be initialled by the parties. Ostensibly bowing to Russian pressure to join the Eurasian Economic Union instead, Yanukovych's decision triggered growing mass protests in the Ukrainian capital that quickly broadened beyond the initial focus on the country's European future and transformed into a more fundamental challenge to Yanukovych's regime and the political and economic situation in Ukraine as a whole and turned into the so-called Maidan revolution (or Revolution of Dignity). As protests continued and the government's response became more heavy-handed and uncompromising at the end of 2013, demands for Yanukovych's resignation grew. A significant escalation of violence at the end of January 2014 led to intensifying negotiations between the parliamentary opposition and the president. Yet, without having a clear mandate from the protesters to do so, the Maidan movement insisted on approving any deal reached in such negotiations. After more than 100 protesters were killed on 18 and 20 February, a deal, mediated by the foreign ministers of Germany, France and Poland (in the presence of an envoy of the Russian president) was brokered between the parliamentary opposition and the President on 21 February, foreseeing a managed transition that would involve constitutional reform and fresh presidential elections before the end of 2014.

Yet, failing to gain the approval by Maidan protesters, this so-called Kyiv agreement was dead in the water within three days of its conclusion. Thus, in this first period between February and April 2014, the agreement on a managed transition immediately failed and events on the ground were perceived as a significant challenge to Russia which saw the disposal of Yanukovych as a major setback (Workshop A).

However, the pro-Western trajectory for which the Maidan partly stood was not universally popular in Ukraine (Workshop A). Rejected by significant parts of the population and political and economic elites, anti-Maidan protests started spontaneously in parts of Donbas. The anti-Western and anti-new regime sentiments that they expressed coincided with Russian security interests and Russia's interpretation of the Maidan as a coup d'etat (Interviews 1, 2). The mere fact of an overlap of interests in Donbas and Moscow, however, did not mean that local elites in Donbas were automatically pro-Russian (Workshop D). Rather as the former governor of Donetsk oblast, Sergey Taruta, noted in a newspaper interview, "Donbas did not agree with the Euromaidan and subsequent decisions by the newly appointed Ukrainian government. But this does not mean that Donbas was on the Kremlin's side. . . . Russia managed the public protests in the way they best served her own interests."[1]

The sudden 'disappearance' of President Yanukovych on 21–22 February 2014 and the subsequent appointment of a new government in Kyiv initially only increased political uncertainty and triggered a near-collapse of the civil service in Ukraine. Since the Ukrainian constitution did not provide for the possibility of presidential impeachment, and given that Yanukovych did not formally resign from his post, the legitimacy of the new government was called into question by its domestic opponents and by Russia. Given that the Euromaidan revolution itself was not universally popular, the new post-Euromaidan government focused on increasing its legitimacy and strengthening its political power domestically by organising democratic elections and entering into a broad dialogue with other Ukrainian elites and externally by building relations with foreign governments, especially with its Western partners in the US and the EU.

In particular, the new government was keen to avoid any confrontations with Yanukovych's former power base. The challenge for the new government was twofold. On the one hand, it needed to assert its control of state institutions, including the civil service and security forces. According to Oleksander Turchinov, acting president of Ukraine after Yanukovych's departure and later on Secretary of the Council of National Security and Defence:

> The first task was to conduct presidential elections openly and transparently in order to secure the legitimacy of the newly appointed Ukrainian government . . . There was widespread sabotage among public servants at all levels. Many of them did not believe that we were able to keep order and political power. They really waited for Russia's invasion and the return of Yanukovych.[2]

The predicament of the new government became even more obvious from the minutes of an urgent meeting of the Council of National Security and

Defence of Ukraine on 28 February 2014, merely one week after Yanukovych's flight to Russia and before the escalation of the crisis in Crimea
and later on in Donbas, which illustrates the general lack of preparedness
of the government and its struggle to assert control,[3] evident also from a
subsequent press release by the National Security and Defence Council of
Ukraine noting that the commander of the Ukrainian navy had been relieved
of his post following a breakdown in the chain of command.[4]

On the other hand, the lack of control over the state's central institutions was further compounded by the fact that Yanukovych's former
supporters also had a potential territorial power base in the Donetsk and
Luhansk oblasts. The refusal of local elites to recognise the legitimacy of
the post-Euromaidan government constituted a serious problem for the new
authorities in Kyiv, as it accelerated the insubordination of local authorities
and prepared the ground for the subsequent fragmentation and chaos that
facilitated the establishment of paramilitary groups which replaced local
Ukrainian authorities (or, in some cases, cooperated with them). In parallel,
informal arrangements concerning local elites' economic assets and financial autonomy also broke down as a result of the general chaos triggered by
the Euromaidan events in Kyiv. The destruction and then protracted restoration of these economic and political power structures became a defining feature of the early stages of the emergence of the future Donetsk and Luhansk
people's republics.

The relative lack of any clear vision for the future among those who now
began to take control in Donbas became apparent from the fact that during
these first months following the victory of the Euromaidan revolution, none
of self-proclaimed leaders of the highly fragmented and mostly spontane-
ous anti-Kyiv/Maidan protests in eastern Ukraine put any specific demands
to the new government in Kyiv (Interviews 4–6). Populistic in their rheto-
ric and relying on pre-existing grievances of the local population, the self-
proclaimed 'people's governors,' 'atamans' and 'commandants' had no
clear idea of a future model of the socio-economic development, adminis-
trative-territorial organisation and governance arrangements in the captured
territories and between them and Kyiv. Rather, they discussed their 'plans'
in vague and utopian terms. For example, Pavel Gubarev, the self-styled
People's Governor of Donetsk, explained that:

> we want to create a fundamentally new state based on social justice and
> equality of people. We now have a chance, an opportunity to reboot. . . .
> When people understand that the new state will protect their rights and
> interests, they will be happy and will support us.[5]

Similarly, Aleksey Mozgovoy, then the commander of the 'Prizrak' battalion of the LPR, stated, "our maximal goals are to overthrow the oligarchic

regime in Kyiv and to build Novorossia . . . life for people, not for oligarchs or politicians."[6]

Such sentiments had already been expressed by some separatist leaders during the early stages of the conflict (Interviews 1–6), and later others expressed similar views when looking back at this period of spring 2014. For example, Pavel Dremov, one of the warlords killed in later power struggles, reflected in late 2014, "we were fighting for a better life for ordinary people against oligarchs and Jews who were robbing us. We fought for Russia and the Soviet Union. I want to ask Russia now – did we fight for cheap humanitarian assistance from you? Or for our ideals?"[7]

Likewise, Aleksandr Zakharchenko, the late prime minister of the DPR, noted that:

> ex-Donetsk oligarchs are like spiders in a bank – they are clinging to their property, do not want to give it up. But they will not succeed. We are building a People's Republic. We will return everything that was stolen to the people.[8]

This problem was clearly recognised in Moscow, as well. Russian President Vladimir Putin's former advisor Gleb Pavlovsky considered the early precursors of today's de-facto states of DPR and LPR stateless as "a vegetative life form of a body without head" and described Moscow's difficulties in coming to terms with this situation:

> informal violence, blurred and uncertain . . . when you cannot understand whom you are dealing with . . . the front without frontline, where paramilitary troops which have uncertain ideologies, forms and territorial allocation, employ both baseball bats and 'Buks.'[9]

The perceived threat of a potential 'loss' of Ukraine, thus, for Moscow, was related to both the replacement of Yanukovych with an anti-Russian, Western-backed government in Kyiv and the Kremlin's own initial inability to exercise sufficient control and coordination over events in Donbas. What was more, it also became clear that the more concerted efforts to keep up the pressure on Kyiv with further anti-Maidan protests in Donbas and other former strongholds of the previous regime such as Kharkiv and Odessa (Interviews 21, 24, 37) failed to get sufficient traction outside Donbas. As a result, Russia began to escalate its involvement in the ongoing 'nomadic occupation' in Donbas by introducing Russian mercenaries, military veterans and private military companies (the most notorious among them being Igor Strelkov, Igor Bezler and the private military company Wagner) into the increasingly anarchical environment in eastern

Ukraine (Interviews 7, 10). In keeping with Moscow's primary goal at the time – destabilisation of southeastern Ukraine in order to increase leverage over the new government on Kyiv – the leaders of these mercenaries did not declare any political goals and did not initiate any negotiations with Kyiv, either. This strategy 'facilitated' the Geneva negotiations and the agreement achieved there in April.[10]

The Joint Statement that resulted from these negotiations was not annulled in the same dramatic way in which the Kyiv Agreement of February 2014 was overtaken by events. There were simply no genuine efforts at its implementation, with all sides offering different interpretations of what the Joint Statement required them to do and in what sequence. Russia was mainly focused on the need for constitutional reform, and admonished Kyiv for exempting anti-rebel militias from the need to disarm,[11] while the Ukrainian government lamented the lack of clarity in the Joint Statement regarding Russian occupation of parts of Donbas and ongoing Russian provocations.[12] As a result, the Ukrainian government resumed its so-called anti-terrorist operation, which, over the following weeks succeeded to a certain extent in rolling back territorial gains made by the rebels (Interview 33). This, in turn, prompted Russia to increase its support to rebels, especially in terms of equipment.

Until the end of July, fighting between Russian-backed rebels and Ukrainian security forces and pro-Ukrainian militias continued and included the downing by rebel forces of a Malaysian Airlines passenger jet, killing all people on board (Dutch Safety Board 2015). Apart from being a major 'PR disaster,' this tragedy also signalled the need to the Kremlin for more control over the rebel forces,[13] and soon after the invasion of so-called vacationers (Russian military personnel 'on leave' from their regular service) began (Interviews 23, 42, 43). During discussions in one of our workshops (Workshop L), one participant noted:

> Russia invaded in Donbas gradually, pushing as far as Ukraine allowed. The government in Kyiv was rather passive. On the one hand, Kyiv did not want to accept Russia's demand for federalization. However, Kyiv also failed to respond adequately by military means to the annexation of Crimea, to Strelkov's operations, and to the invasion of 'vacationers.' Ultimately, Kyiv's passivity encouraged Russia to increase the stakes.

This dynamic of increasing Russian involvement in Donbas is the focus of our next two chapters. We begin with an analysis of the identity dynamics of the conflict before we turn to the more focused and systematic state-building efforts that were conducted by Moscow from the summer of 2014 onwards. The two processes, while we keep them analytically separate in the following, are, of course, closely intertwined. Together, they form part of the parameters within which, ultimately, the feasibility and viability of any conflict settlement will be deter.

Notes

1 Authors' translation from www.gazeta.zn.ua/internal/sergey-taruta-dazhe-esli-shahterov-ispolzuyut-eto-ne-isklyuchaet-ih-realnyh-problem-nuzhen-dialog-a-ne-ultimatumy.html.

2 See "Aleksander Turchinov: Ya Ob'yavlyayu Mobilizatsiyu, a Mne govoryat chto Ya Provotsiruyu Russkih", *Censor.Net*, 1 March 2017, https://censor.net.ua/resonance/429784/aleksandr_turchinov_obyavlyayu_mobilizatsiyu_a_mne_partnery_govoryat_chto_ya_provotsiruyu_russkih (accessed 24 September 2018); "Турчинов про весну 2014 року: Були пропозиції запровадити воєнний стан і керувати країною необмежений час Більше читайте тут", https://gordonua.com/ukr/news/politics/turchinov-pro-vesnu-2014-roku-buli-propozitsiji-zaprovaditi-vijskovij-stan-i-keruvati-krajinoju-neobmezhenij-chas-176571.html (accessed 24 September 2018).

3 See "Про невідкладні заходи щодо забезпечення національної безпеки, суверенітету і територіальної цілісності України", Документ n0001525–14, чинний, поточна редакція – Введення в дію від 03.03.2014, підстава 189/2014, http://zakon.rada.gov.ua/laws/show/n0001525-14 (accessed 24 September 2018).

4 See "Заступник Секретаря РНБОУ В. Сюмар: Д. Березовського відсторонено від посади командувача ВМС України", Staff of the National Security and Defence Council of Ukraine, 2 March 2014, www.rnbo.gov.ua/news/1588.html (accessed 24 September 2018).

5 "Self-styled people's governor of Donetsk tells us: These areas have always been Russian", Interview with Pavel Gubarev, https://theconversation.com/self-styled-peoples-governor-of-donetsk-tells-us-these-areas-have-always-been-russian-29708 (accessed 24 September 2018).

6 "Один из лидеров ЛНР: Мы хотим взять Киев и свергнуть олигархический строй", Interview with Aleksey Mozgovoy, 1 September 2014, https://regnum.ru/news/polit/1842532.html (accessed 24 September 2018).

7 "Павел Дремов: Плотницкого в отставку!", Statement by Pavel Dremov, 29 December 2014, www.youtube.com/watch?v=mRV7ShdS5Z8 (accessed 24 September 2018).

8 TV-show 'Chay s Zakharom' (Moderator: Zakhar Prilepin), Tzargrad TV, Interview with Aleksander Zakharchenko, 5 December 2016, www.youtube.com/watch?v=NHTeTZiqVRw&list=PLoakhgttSsPoE9VwoCu-MdZF4FU7-GswR&index=37 (accessed 24 September 2018).

9 "Глеб Павловский: Путин уже наигрался в единоличного преемника . . .", Interview with Gleb Pavlovsky, 31 August 2016, https://sobesednik.ru/dmitriy-bykov/20160831-gleb-pavlovskiy-putin-uzhe-naigralsya-v-edinolichnogo-preemn (accessed 24 September 2018).

10 This view of the sequence of events is broadly shared among local and international observers (Interview 8; Interview 16; Interview 17; Workshop J).

11 See statements by Russian Foreign Minister Sergey Lavrov as reported by Interfax: "Лавров: власти Киева не выполняют и грубо нарушают женевские договоренности", 21 April 2014, www.interfax.ru/world/372850 (accessed 24 September 2018); and "Россия обвинила Украину в затягивании конституционной реформы", 21 April 2014, www.interfax.ru/world/372853 (accessed 24 September 2018); as well as "Глеб Павловский: Путин уже наигрался в единоличного преемника . . .", Interview with Gleb Pavlovsky, 31 August 2016, https://sobesednik.ru/dmitriy-bykov/20160831-gleb-pavlovskiy-putin-uzhe-naigralsya-v-edinolichnogo-preemn (accessed 24 September 2018).

12 "Женевские соглашения не дали ответов на многие вопросы – Турчинов", Interview with acting President of Ukraine Oleksandr Turchynov, 20 April 2014, http://news.liga.net/news/politics/1445766-zhenevskie_soglasheniya_ ostavili_mnogie_voprosy_otkrytymi_turchinov.htm (accessed 24 September 2018).

13 In Summer 2014, Russian nationals took over key positions in Donbas and a team of 'officials' from Transnistria were drafted in to use their experience of (de-facto) state-building.

4 Identity and identity-building in Donbas before and after the beginning of the conflict

Building on our analysis of the origins and evolution of the crisis in Ukraine until the summer of 2014 that we offered in the preceding chapter, we now turn our attention to what is often referred to as Donbas or Donetsk identity and the efforts to shape and reshape it over the course of Ukraine's independence since 1991. As such, this chapter provides a crucial link between our discussion of the origins and early developments of the conflict between late 2013 and mid-2014, and the examination of the more focused and systematic state-building efforts undertaken by Moscow from summer 2014 onwards. Our argument here connects these two distinct phases in the development of the overall crisis in Ukraine by demonstrating how an apparently solid nested identity that allowed strong local and regional identities to co-exist with an overall national Ukrainian identity began to crumble under the pressure of an ensuing civil war and thus created both opportunity and need for Moscow and its local allies in Donbas to extend and consolidate their gains by simultaneously intensifying military hostilities against Ukrainian forces and building more viable de-facto states in the rebel-controlled territories.

Nested identities in post-independence Ukraine

One of the striking features of identity in Ukraine for many years has been the importance of local and regional identities alongside a national identity and the comparatively easy 'co-existence' of these multiple, layered identities. This has been the case across all of Ukraine's regions, with relatively few differences between them prior to the outbreak of the crisis in late 2013. An opinion poll in 2005, for example, found that more than 50% of residents of eastern Ukraine, including in the Donetsk and Luhansk oblasts, considered themselves first as residents of their hometown (37%) or region (19%), and 32% saw Ukraine as a whole as the primary reference point for their identity as a whole. While the principal fault-line in Ukrainian politics is now often seen between eastern and western regions of the country, these differences – however pronounced they may have become over the past five years – were barely noticeable back in 2005, when residents of western Ukraine responded in quite similar ways: 38.5% considering themselves first as residents of their hometown, 15% as residents of their region, and 34% as residents of Ukraine as a whole.[1] Two years later, when asked whether they perceived Ukraine as their homeland, 91% of respondents in the eastern parts of Ukraine did so, compared to just under 98% in western parts,[2] while 60% and 71% of respondents in eastern and western Ukraine, respectively, disagreed with the suggestion that "political, linguistic, cultural and economic differences between the western and eastern regions of Ukraine" were so profound "that in the long run they can separate and create their own states or join other states."[3]

This embeddedness of a national Ukrainian identity in local and regional identities and the comparative lack of political salience, at the time, of allegedly more divisive ethnic identities,[4] helps to understand that, while there was some support in Donbas for unification of Ukraine with Russia, an independent Ukraine was still the preference of an overwhelming majority of the population in these arguably most pro-Russian regions of Ukraine (Workshops D, F). However, it is important to note the impact of even the early days of the crisis on these views: according to an opinion poll conducted in February 2014, 33% of residents in Donetsk and 24% in Luhansk favoured unification of Ukraine as a whole with Russia.[5] This represented a marked increase from a poll conducted in December 2013. While not directly comparable in terms of reference group, asked whether their region should separate from Ukraine and join another state, only 8.9% of respondents in the eastern region favoured such a course of action,[6] a figure that had actually decreased by 2.5 percentage points compared to responses to an identical question back in 2007.[7]

These polling data do not present a conclusive picture of identity dynamics in Ukraine as a whole, or any of its regions. However, even as a series of more or less comparable snapshots, they demonstrate that there was no deeply entrenched, widespread anti-Ukrainian sentiment in the eastern parts of the country or persistent separatist tendencies, but also that an overall pro-Ukrainian sentiment was relatively volatile to external 'shocks,' as indicated by developments in and after the beginning of the crisis in late 2013. In order to understand these dynamics and examine their impact on subsequent developments, it is useful to consider the evolution of a Donbas identity, and more specifically the Donetsk identity since Ukraine's independence in 1991.

After the collapse of the Soviet Union, the Donetsk province of Ukraine became a part of so-called 'red belt' – a number of Ukrainian provinces in which a leftist ideology dominated and manifested itself in persistently strong electoral performances of communist and socialist parties. The so-called 'Donetsk' identity – a strong regional identification embedded within an overall Ukrainian national identity – had emerged as a result of the initial competition between, and eventual convergence of, post-independence political-economic Donetsk elites and the communist and socialist parties that survived, or emerged from, the collapse of Soviet party structures. This process occurred in the course of a number of policy and media projects aimed at the creation of a unified societal area in Donbas since the early 1990s (Interviews 58, 60, 61). Twenty-five years later and following the crisis since late 2013, however, this Donetsk identity has lost most of its former dominance in the Ukrainian-controlled territories of the Donetsk and Luhansk regions, and the indications are that this is also the case in the rebel-controlled areas.[8] In the following, we therefore trace the rise and fall of this Ukrainian-Donbas identity, thus providing a crucial component of the background against which we can subsequently explain the nature and, so far, relative success of the Russian-supported and directed separatist state-building effort in the emerging de-facto entities of DPR and LPR.

Building a local identity in Donbas in post-independence Ukraine, 1991–2013

Identity-building efforts in Donbas before the outbreak of the crisis in late 2013 were entirely domestically focused and aimed at the consolidation of a local electorate during the Ukrainian elections behind political parties controlled by locally dominant elites (Interviews 55, 60, 61). At the time, the population of the entire Donetsk and Luhansk oblasts of Ukraine numbered around seven million people, resulting in over 20% of the 450 MPs of the Verkhovna Rada, thus giving local elites significant influence at the centre and some bargaining power to obtain a degree of local fiscal autonomy. Yet, the latter was always much more of an elite-driven project and popular among the local Ukrainian elites of economically developed provinces of Ukraine in general (Interviews 49, 51). Moreover, the 'Donetsk' identity that emerged constituted a form of Ukrainian civic identity, similar to regional Ukrainian identities in other peripheral provinces of Ukraine with a rich history, such as Odessa and Lviv (Interviews 49, 51, 54). Thus, prior to 2014, the establishment of an independent Donbas 'state' had never been the goal of any identity-building project in Donbas.[9]

However, several distinct factors shaped the way in which Donetsk regional identity was created and the kind of identity that emerged and, in turn, provided the foundation for popular mobilisation in response to the events on the Maidan in Kyiv in 2013–2014 and during the further evolution of the conflict in Donbas. The first relevant factor in this context is the loss of the Soviet identity after the collapse of Soviet Union, combined with deepening socio-economic inequalities – vertically between different social strata in newly independent Ukraine and horizontally between different provinces, primarily between the industrial east and the rural west (Interview 25). Second, and similar to other post-Soviet countries, new economic elites emerged in Donbas in the course of the privatisation of Soviet economic assets. It took several severe criminal wars (which other Ukrainian provinces did not experience) before a stable Donetsk 'clan,' with Yanukovych as one of its leaders, emerged and, over time, consolidated itself as a political-economic entity, integrating representatives of the 'red directors corporation,' young oligarchs, local bureaucracy, and criminal groups (Interviews 51, 52). The core of the Donetsk clan's business were export-oriented metal production enterprises and chemicals, the competitiveness of which critically depended on the price of Russian natural gas and access to European markets.

The Party of the Regions, led by Yanukovych, became the local elites' political arm behind which they rallied the electorate of Donetsk and Luhansk oblasts, thus obtaining their significant bargaining power in Kyiv, used to lobby for local elite interests and to give expression and representation of popular norms and values embodied in the notion of 'Donetsk' identity based on shared interests.

A critical element of these interests was the demand for the maintenance of socio-economic and cultural ties with Russia, which became a central point of the Party of Regions' political agenda (Interviews 59, 62, 63). The gradual, yet ultimately successful, realignment of the electorate is apparent from the following figures. In the 1998 parliamentary elections, the Party of the Regions (under its then name Party of Regional Renaissance) received less than 1% of the vote nationwide and about 2% of the popular vote in Donetsk oblast. In 2002, the share of the vote won by the electoral block 'For a United Ukraine,' of which the Party of the Regions was then a part, had grown to about 40% in Donetsk, with a nationwide average of 11.77% in the PR vote and a total of thirty-five members of parliament (MPs) elected under the plural constituency vote. In 2006, running on its own, the Party of the Regions won just under 74% in Donetsk and 32% nationwide, making it the party with the single largest share of the popular vote and paving the way to Yanukovych's win in the 2010 presidential elections against Yuliya Timoshenko.[10]

The emergence and political success of this Donetsk regional identity, however, cannot be seen in isolation from post-Soviet identity formation processes elsewhere in Ukraine. The growth of Ukrainian nationalism and Ukrainian nationalist movements and political parties in Western Ukraine, with their simultaneous pro-European (i.e., pro-Western) orientation, was an important contributing factor in the polarisation of Ukraine and the emergence of the so-called 'two Ukraines.' This concept considers the population of Donbas as an outpost for Soviet, eastern Slavonic, paternalist identity, closely tied to the 'Russian World' as opposed to the European identity embraced by western Ukrainians.[11] However, this idea of 'two Ukraines' glosses over the core difference between eastern and western Ukrainian elites which manifests itself in their opposite visions of Ukrainian statehood. Eastern Ukrainian elites ('Donetskie,' 'Kharkovskie,' 'Dnipropetrovskie') advocated a Ukraine privileging regions vis-à-vis the centre, whereas western Ukrainian elites were, and remain, more focused on strengthening the centre vis-à-vis regions. As noted earlier in the context of the gradual emergence of the Donetsk identity after 1991, even though these were elite-driven and elite-serving projects, they managed to incorporate, and give expression to, popular views and thus create regional bases for themselves, which, in turn, sustained and over time increased perceptions of geographically based differences similar to those expressed in the 'two Ukraines' concept. While not immediately evident from polling data until the beginning of the crisis in 2013, the rapid and momentous changes triggered by the Maidan protests provided the catalyst for these differences to become increasingly irreconcilable where previously national, regional and local identities and interests could be integrated and managed, and co-exist.

While it would be short-sighted to underestimate the significance of Donetsk elites' pragmatic, rather than culturally based, interest in closer ties and cooperation with Russia, the cultural dimension of Donetsk identity became an important reference point in the political mobilisation of Donbas in the early stages of the conflict and thereafter. This, in turn, needs to be seen in the context of the campaign of perceived Ukrainiansation of eastern Ukraine that then president Victor Yushchenko started after the victory of the Orange Revolution in 2005. Aimed at the promotion of the Ukrainian language, culture and national identity in education, media and public life in Ukraine more generally, Yushchenko's government introduced policies that required the obligatory translation of foreign media reports and TV shows into Ukrainian, the use of the Ukrainian language in public service, schools and education, particularly in eastern Ukrainian provinces and Crimea.[12] After the victory of Viktor Yanukovych in the 2010 presidential elections, many of these policies were abandoned and changes previously introduced were undone, with the result that the Russian language returned to its previous status.[13] Yet, taken together, Yushchenko's policies and their reversal by Yanukovych contributed to the growing public sense of 'two Ukraines.'

What is important to bear in mind in all this, however, is that the Donetsk identity project remained a predominantly Ukrainian project in the sense that its political and economic foundations and objectives were focused on the nature of the Ukrainian state and its relationship with its principal international partners and reference points – Russia and Europe, respectively – and not on the break-up of the country (Interviews 25, 26, 60, 61). This is clearly demonstrated in opinion polls carried out over the past several years, which show consistently that residents of Donbas identified with both their region and Ukraine (see previous). In this sense, until the beginning of the crisis in late 2013, 'two Ukraines' symbolised a struggle of two competing visions of the nature of Ukrainian statehood, rather than the separatist conflict it has turned into subsequently.

This transformation above all demonstrates that the construct of a nested Donbas-Ukrainian identity did not prove resilient over the course of the conflict from late 2013 onwards. The initial developments – parallel local-local and state-local conflicts – already signalled the dependence of the political relevance of a local Donbas identity on the presence of local elites mobilising forces in its defence. This, as we demonstrate ahead, made it critical for Russia to force established local elites out of the territories it occupied, which, once successful, led to the disappearance of this Donbas-Ukrainian identity as a politically salient identity – however, without establishing as yet a sustainable alternative.

The transformation of identity after the beginning of the conflict

The military conflict in eastern Ukraine has triggered the consolidation of Ukrainian national identity on government-controlled territories. While this takes the form of decidedly anti-Russian identity in parts of central and western Ukraine, this is not the case in eastern Ukraine, but here, too, the sense of a Ukrainian national identity has been strengthened. As Maria Zolkina from the Foundation for Democratic Initiatives observed in an interview in October 2016,

> before the conflict began, Donetsk and Lugansk regions were primarily internally oriented. The percentage of people with a regional and local identity in the Donbass was the highest in the country . . . after the beginning of military events in 2014, the number of people seeing themselves first as a citizen of Ukraine gradually began to grow. To date, around two-thirds of residents in the Ukrainian-controlled part of the Donbass primarily call themselves citizens of Ukraine.[14]

By contrast, interviews with internally displaced persons (IDPs) from Donbas and pro-Russian fighters demonstrate that self-identification of residents in the rebel-controlled territories is blurred and fluid (Interviews 45–48, 50, 51, 54, 55).[15] This is due to a number of factors.

First, before 2014, the Donetsk and Luhansk oblasts of Ukraine were socially and economically well-integrated, as well as united politically behind the Party of the Region and the Yanukovych clan which controlled it (Mikheeva 2014). As soon as the border between the self-declared republics and Ukrainian-controlled territories stabilised, residents of these different entities found themselves under the influence of forces with clearly divergent agendas and were consequently exposed to conflicting information and ideology promotion policies, leading to a significant degree of alienation and fragmentation of society in Donbas as it existed before the conflict as well as further polarisation between rebel-controlled and government-controlled parts of Ukraine (Interviews 7, 8, 41, 44). This has been partly facilitated by the profound social upheaval during the conflict, leading to the flight of entire social strata (economic elites, bureaucracy, middle class, creative class, students and intelligentsia) from Donbas (Horbulin 2016). The resulting vacuum created the space for the 'construction' of new identities that were significantly shaped by both the wartime experiences of the population in Donbas on both sides of the front line and the subsequent establishment and institutional entrenchment of mutually exclusive narratives of these experiences by opposing political regimes (weak democracy in Ukraine and military dictatorship/warlordism in DPR/LPR), through exposure to conflicting information policies (Ukrainian versus Russian propaganda), and by way of education programmes that emphasise, often irreconcilable, differences among people (Interviews 47, 56).

What is important to bear in mind in this context is that the fragmentation of the Donbas identity is not only a question of divergence between Ukrainian-controlled and rebel-controlled territories, but also affects the rebel-controlled territories themselves for a number of reasons. First, as soon as the initial leftist project of state-building failed to get any serious traction, there began intensive, but ultimately unsystematic and contradictory, efforts to construct a new Donbas identity. These efforts were informed by various ideas: the unity of Donbas, the claim that Donbas is part of the so-called 'Russian world', or that the DPR and LPR should eventually be reintegrated into Ukraine. Yet, none of these 'visions' have so far been coherently articulated as a viable political project. For example, Zakhar Prilepin, one of the authors of the Malorossia project, considers that the "DPR and LPR are a trap through which Russia keeps Ukraine in its orbit. If we tear out DPR/LPR, Ukraine will drift into another direction . . . and we will not be able to keep it under our influence."[16]

Gleb Pavlovsky, a former adviser to President Putin, notes that "Malorossia is a project of reconstruction of the Ukrainian state."[17] While this is consistent, to some extent, with Prilepin's idea of DPR and LPR as levers of influence over Kyiv, rebel leader Igor Strelkov stated that "serious implementation of Malorossia and other similar projects means full-fledged war against Ukraine."[18]

Western observers highlight the improbable nature of the Malorossia project and emphasise how disconnected it appears from realities on the ground and how much it posed an obstacle to the implementation of the (first) Minsk Accord.[19]

Similar scepticism was expressed by Russian politician Eduard Limonov who appears convinced that "Malorossia will not succeed . . . its fate will be similar to the fate of other intellectual adventures like Novorossia. These antiquated notions have nothing in common with realities in contemporary Donbas."[20]

But what are these realities? At present, there is no coherent identity-building project in Donbas. Attempts to create a new Donbas identity compete with partially incompatible notions of Malorossia and Novorossia that remain prominent in an attempt to project a coherent image of the Russian World (Russkii Mir). Efforts to connect Donbas (Malorossia, Novorossia) with Russia (Velikorossia) and to link the three 'brother nations' of Russia, Ukraine and Belarus by appealing to a Soviet and imperial Russian past, however, sit uneasily alongside political aspirations to enable Moscow to influence Kyiv through an eventual reintegration of Donbas into Ukraine (Interview 31).

As one of our interlocutors explained:

> The task for new a identity-building project would be difficult. It has to explain why the population of Donbas should fight against Kyiv, but also why Russia cannot annex Donetsk and Luhansk. The new 'People of Donbas' have to be non-Ukrainians, but friendly to Russia.
>
> (Interview 25)

At the same time, there are some local developments that stimulate, and shape, the process of identity formation in the rebel-controlled areas of Donbas. These are primarily associated with local grievances both towards Kyiv and Moscow, and thus define any newly emerging identity in terms of what it is not. Local grievances towards Ukraine are associated with peoples' wartime experience (especially shelling by Ukrainian armed forces and pro-government militias), blockades, discrimination against IDPs from Donbas in Ukrainian-controlled territories and hate speech by Ukrainian politicians and media directed at remaining residents. Yet, anti-Kyiv sentiments have not translated into pro-Moscow sentiments. On the contrary, local grievances are also directed at Russia. They are linked to the unwillingness to protect an unfavourable comparison of Russia's policy towards Donbas and Crimea – i.e., the absence of a credible Crimean scenario for Donbas, and a perception that Donbas is simply used as a pawn to provide the Kremlin with additional leverage over Kyiv – its discrimination of refugees from Donbas in Russia, and the socio-economic decline in Donetsk and Luhansk. The sense of being abandoned and/or used by both Ukraine and Russia creates conditions that could be conducive to the re-emergence of a new local identity. This is further facilitated, to some extent, by the fact that local residents are almost equally disillusioned with their 'republican' elites who are locally still perceived as Ukrainian, rather than Russian, elites because they display a similarly predatory behaviour and are considered 'inherited' from the previous Ukrainian system. As one of our local interlocutors noted:

> The appointment of ex-Ukrainian public officials and members of the Party of Regions to higher positions in the DPR's government exacerbates the development of protest attitudes among the population of DPR. There is a perception that Ukrainian representatives hold political power in Donetsk.
>
> (Interview 65)

After the assassination of DPR leader Aleksander Zakharchenko at the end of August 2018, local media in the self-declared republics and Russian mass media published what they referred to as evidence of economic crimes committed by the government of the DPR, including racketeering, extortion, smuggling and kidnapping, as well as corruption on a grand scale.[21] While the assassination of Zakharchenko was attributed, as usual, by the Kremlin to Ukrainian and Western intelligence services, it does, however, demonstrate how tenuous Moscow's control of the local elites in the self-declared republics can be at times. Much like the successful coup – a year prior to Zakharchenko's assassination – against his LPR counterpart Igor Plotnitskiy, it also demonstrated the continued existence and relevance of the Donetskiye's 'deep state' – the organised criminal networks that have been influential power brokers in Donbas since the 1990s.

More recently, however, the Kremlin has once again tried to assert more control over local politics. Aleksander Khodakovsky, a former commander of the Ukrainian anti-terrorist battalion 'Alfa' and of the DPR's 'Vostok' battalion, had been an outspoken and locally popular critic of former DPR leader Zakharchenko. With Zakharchenko dead, his chances in the upcoming elections in the DPR had dramatically improved. Yet, he was prevented from entering the DPR from Russia's side of the border by Russian board guards, in an obvious attempt to stop him from participating in the elections. This is both evidence of Russia's continuing policy to limit the influence of the 'old' Donetskiye in Donbas and push their own preferred 'new' candidates, in this case the locally less popular Denis Pushilin,[22] and the continuing infighting among local elites. Because Khodakovsky has, to some extent, a power base of his own in terms of the local support he enjoys and his pre-existing strong links with Ukrainian economic elites, and is thus less dependent on Russia, there is a possible danger here for Moscow that he might negotiate a reintegration deal for the self-declared republics into Ukraine without Russia.[23] While Russia is not in principle opposed to reintegration, it requires, as we noted above, terms for such reintegration that would guarantee the Kremlin's long-term influence in and on Kyiv, which is easier to achieve if Moscow retains control over key personnel in the self-declared republics.

It is difficult to assess the sustainability of the process of building a new 'national' Donbas identity, as it competes with remnants of the old Donetsk identity and various equally incompatible notions of Donbas as part of Novrossiya, Malorossiya or the Russian World. While our direct observations suggest that there is some optimism among local residents regarding the future of the Donetsk and Luhansk people's republics, efforts to mould a new identity in the rebel-controlled areas have so far not gained significant traction. For example, although there are no open source opinion polls on the situation in the self-declared republics, the Ministry of Information Policy of Ukraine has recently accepted that at least 18% residents of Donetsk and Luhansk consider themselves as 'citizens of DPR or LPR,' whereas another 60% stick to an (old) regional version of 'Donetsk' identity.[24]

Yet, the conditions, borne of the specific circumstances in which people in rebel-controlled areas find themselves, in which such a new 'national' Donetsk identity could grow and be embraced by an increasing number of local residents are clearly there. Living in a zone of armed conflict, frequently migrating between the rebel-controlled and Ukrainian-controlled territories, and having family or business ties on both sides of the front line, the daily struggle for individual survival dominates local residents' everyday life practices, and they adjust to the rules of whichever political regime is more relevant to them at a specific time and in a concrete place. As the majority of the rebel-controlled population belongs to this group, it is easy to see why the old Ukrainian-Donbas identity, in which local and national identities co-existed, eroded quickly and why, as yet, no sustainable 'replacement' has emerged. But, if anything, the direction of travel seems clear. As one of our interlocutors, who identifies himself as 'belonging to Donetsk identity,' explains:

> What was the difference between us and western Ukrainians? We have always considered ourselves self-sufficient while western Ukrainians

kneeled before Poles and other Europeans. Now Russians want us to feel inferior towards them, and that is equally unacceptable.

(Interview 65)

Incoherent and inclusive as they may have been so far, local identity-building efforts have not been without consequences. Regardless of which agenda they have pursued, none of these efforts are acceptable to the current government in Kyiv or, in fact, to the vast majority of the population in Ukraine. Donbas and its remaining residents had initially in part been perceived as victims of circumstances, but this perception has gradually shifted to seeing them as separatist, anti-Ukrainian, anti-European, and pro-Russian (Interviews 11, 45–48). This, in turn, has hardened attitudes against any form of special status for these areas in a future constitutional settlement. The resulting policy of isolation pursued by Kyiv, together with the political regime of military dictatorship and Russian military presence in Donbas, ironically, is likely to contribute not only to the consolidation of Russian influence (albeit not to widespread pro-Russian sentiments, as noted previously) but also to the emergence, over time, of a new and potentially sustainable identity that will exhibit all the hallmarks of separatist, anti-Ukrainian, anti-European, and pro-Russian attitudes. This self-fulfilling prophecy in the making, in turn, will have a significant impact on future settlement scenarios.

Importantly, the old Ukrainian-Donbas identity has also been under pressure outside the rebel-controlled areas of Donbas. Since the start of the war in Donbas, there has been a process of stratification of 'old' Donetsk elites leading to a weakening of their public support and position vis-à-vis political opponents in Kyiv, Donetsk and Luhansk. The most important driving force for this has been the loss of their political power and economic assets in their traditional strongholds – Crimea and Donbas – and the establishment of the Russian state and Russia-backed authorities there.

In the meantime, the main electoral base of the 'Opposition Bloc' – a successor to the Party of Regions – is located in Ukrainian-controlled parts of Donbas and southeastern Ukraine (Zaporizhzhya and Dnipro oblasts). According to opinion polls,[25] the 'Opposition Bloc' enjoys its largest support in municipalities of eastern Ukraine, and its informal leader and representative of the remaining Donetskiye, Rinat Akhmetov, is the most popular leader in Ukraine-controlled Donbas (49% of support, compared with 10% for President Poroshenko).[26]

As a parliamentary faction, the 'Opposition Bloc' unites representatives of big Ukrainian business and opposes the socio-cultural policies of the Ukrainian government, but widely cooperates with the government on economic policy, frequently via corruption networks. For example, the so-called 'Rotterdam Plus' deal negotiated by Poroshenko facilitated the rise of state-controlled prices for coal, supplied from coal-mining enterprises of DTEK (owned by Rinat Akhmetov) in exchange for DTEK's Eurobonds (granted to Poroshenko's company).[27] As a result of such cooperation, Akhmetov is the only oligarch who increased his income during Poroshenko's tenure, thus compensating him to some extent for the loss of his assets in rebel-controlled Donbas. Akhmetov's personal success in protecting his position notwithstanding, the old Donetskiye, having slowly restored and consolidated their influence in Ukraine-controlled Mariupol, Kramatorsk and Zapoizhzhya through investments into the local economy and social infrastructure, still face problems with uniting the many different and smaller local political factions to counterbalance western Ukrainian elites in the Ukrainian parliament and government.

As a result, compared to their position before the beginning of the crisis in 2013, there is an overall weakening of eastern Ukrainian elites' position the country as a whole, further exacerbated by the economic decline in the previously wealthy industrialised regions of Kharkiv, Donetsk and Luhansk. In addition, the territorial divisions imposed on Donbas as a consequence of the violent conflict there have also pitted the 'old' Donbas identity still present, albeit much weakened, in some of the Ukraine-controlled territories against the so-called 'new' Donbas identity which is beginning to emerge in the rebel-controlled territories.

If the current trends continue, including the flight of capital and skills from rebel-controlled parts of Donbas, the past socio-economic disproportions between 'wealthy' Donetsk city (the socio-economic and political capital of Donbas) and other poorer territories of Luhansk and Donetsk oblasts would be decreasing in a spatial sense within rebel-controlled territories, while still depriving Ukraine-controlled Donbas of a credible centre. Further lack of investment into war-affected territories of Donbas, continuing de-industrialisation, persistently low levels of income, emigration and predatory elites will contribute to the marginalisation of the DPR and LPR-controlled territories of Donbas from both Ukraine as a whole and Ukrainian-controlled Donbas. Taken together, these developments already have contributed to the marginalisation of eastern Ukraine, including in terms of its political representation in, and influence on, the central government. As they are likely to continue to do so in the future, they, too, will have a profound impact on any potential conflict settlement.

Notes

1 See poll of 2009 respondents conducted by the Razumkov Center in December 2005 in all regions of Ukraine. http://old.razumkov.org.ua/ukr/poll.php?poll_id=762 (accessed 24 September 2018).

2   See poll of 10,956 respondents conducted by the Razumkov Center in May and June 2007 in all regions of Ukraine. http://old.razumkov.org.ua/ukr/poll.php?poll_id=775 (accessed 24 September 2018).

3   See poll of 10,956 respondents conducted by the Razumkov Center in May and June 2007 in all regions of Ukraine. http://old.razumkov.org.ua/ukr/poll.php?poll_id=736 (accessed 24 September 2018).

4   According to the 2001 census, the proportion of ethnic Ukrainians and ethnic Russians in Donetsk and Luhansk oblasts was approximately 60:40.

5   See "Dinamika stavlennya naselennya Ukraïni do Rosiï ta naselennya Rosiï do Ukraïni, yakih vidnosin z Rosieyu hotili b ukraïntsi", poll of 2032 respondents conducted in February 2014 by the Kyiv International Institute of Sociology. http://kiis.com.ua/?lang=ukr&cat=reports&id=236&page=1 (accessed 24 September 2018). Support for this option was highest in Crimea (41%), with substantial minorities also in favour in Odessa (24%), Zaporozhye (17%), and Kharkiv (15%).

6   See poll of 2010 respondents conducted by the Razumkov Center in December 2013 in all regions of Ukraine. http://old.razumkov.org.ua/ukr/poll.php?poll_id=934 (accessed 24 September 2018).

7   See poll of 10,956 respondents conducted by the Razumkov Center in May and June 2007 in all regions of Ukraine. http://old.razumkov.org.ua/ukr/poll.php?poll_id=318 (accessed 24 September 2018).

8   See "Переселенці з Донбасу перетворилися на кочівників", www.radiosvoboda.org/a/27412454.html (accessed 24 September 2018).

9   This is also evident from the opinion polls cited earlier.

10 All data from the website of the Central Electoral Commission of Ukraine at www.cvk.gov.ua/ (accessed 24 September 2018).

11 Yet, Mykola Riabchuk, who coined the term of 'two Ukraines' back in 1992, also notes that "both rival groups, 'russophile' and 'ukrainophile' (or, more precisely, pro-Soviet and pro-European) are minorities, while the real majority is an amorphous group of those who 'do not care', 'are not interested', 'feel undecided', and 'failed' (or 'refused') to respond." See "Ukraine: One state, two countries?", www.iwm.at/transit/transit-online/ukraine-one-state-two-countries/ (accessed 24 September 2018).

12 See Decree of the President of Ukraine No. 1122/2007 "On some measures on the development of the humanitarian sphere in the Autonomous Republic of Crimea and Sevastopol", www.president.gov.ua/documents/11222007-6687 (accessed 24 September 2018).

13 See Law "On foundations of state language policy", *Bulletin of the Verkhovna Rada (VVR)*, 2013, No. 23, p. 218, http://zakon.rada.gov.ua/laws/show/5029-17 (accessed 24 September 2018).

14 See "Большинство жителей подконтрольной части Донбасса считает себя украинцами", Interview with Maria Zolkina, 12 October 2016, http://dif.org.ua/article/bolshinstvo-zhiteley-podkontrolnoy-chasti-donbassa-schitaet-sebya-ukraintsami (accessed 24 September 2018).

15 See also Malyarenko and Galbreath (2016).

16 See "Программа 'Без галстуков': Писатель Захар Прилепин", 8 December 2016, www.youtube.com/watch?v=YQeNUuI7TYc (accessed 24 September 2018); see also "В гостях у Захара Прилепина Константин Малофеев", 9 April 2017, www.youtube.com/watch?v=G0OaeuarBr8&list=PLoakhgttSsPoE9VwoCu-MdZF4FU7-GswR&index=19 (accessed 24 September 2018), and

"Захар Прилепин: я пришел в Москву как приходили князья из кавказских окраин", *Daily Storm*, 2 July 2018, https://dailystorm.ru/vlast/zahar-prilepin-ya-prishel-v-moskvu-kak-prihodili-voennye-knyazya-s-kavkazskih-okrain (accessed 24 September 2018).

17 "Глеб Павловский: Путин уже наигрался в единоличного преемника . . .", Interview with Gleb Pavlovsky, 31 August 2016, https://sobesednik.ru/dmitriy-bykov/20160831-gleb-pavlovskiy-putin-uzhe-naigralsya-v-edinolichnogo-preemn (accessed 24 September 2018).

18 "Игорь Стрелков: что это было? Движение 'Новороссия Игоря Стрелкова'", 19 July 2017, http://novorossia.pro/strelkov/3799-igor-strelkov-chto-eto-bylo.html (accessed 24 September 2018).

19 "Проект 'Малороссия': зачем сепаратистам на Украине понадобился ребрендинг?", *DW*, 18 July 2017, www.dw.com/ru/проект-малороссия-зачем-сепаратистам-на-украине-понадобился-ребрендинг/39739033 (accessed 24 September 2018). For a good overview of such criticisms, see "Ukraine separatist 'Little Russia' sparks concern over peace deal", *Deutsche Welle*, 18 July 2017, www.dw.com/en/ukraine-separatist-little-russia-sparks-concern-over-peace-deal/a-39743870 (accessed 24 September 2018).

20 See "Эдуард Лимонов о Малороссии", *Regnum*, 20 July 2017, https://regnum.ru/news/2303451.html (accessed 24 September 2018).

21 See, for example, "Ненасытные", *Новая Газета*, 3 September 2018, www.novayagazeta.ru/articles/2018/09/02/77684-nenasytnye (accessed 24 September 2018). In September 2018, temporary investigative commission to investigate economic crimes made by Zakharchenko's government was established by parliament of DPR, https://dnrsovet.su/vremennaya-komissiya-po-vyyavleniyu-faktov-protivopravnoj-deyatelnosti-mds-provela-pervoe-rabochee-zasedanie/ (accessed 24 September 2018).

22 See "Ставка на Пушилина и аресты 'бывших'. Журналист рассказал о тайном совещании руководства 'ДНР' в Ростове", *Strana.UA*, 11 September 2018, https://strana.ua/news/160589-v-rostove-surkov-provel-sekretnoe-soveshchanie-po-budushchemu-ldnr.html (accessed 24 September 2018).

23 See "Не выпустили из России. Ходаковский не примет участие в 'выборах' в 'ДНР'", *Strana.UA*, 21 September 2018, https://strana.ua/news/162339-aleksandr-khodakovskij-ne-smozhet-prinjat-uchastie-v-vyborakh-hlavy-dnr.html (accessed 24 September 2018).

24 See "Особливості свідомості та ідентичності жителів окупованої та підконтрольної території Донецької та Луганської області: аналітичний звіт, 2018", Міністерство інформаційної політики, https://mip.gov.ua/files/pdf/ ПРЕЗЕНТАЦІЯ_соціологія_2018_Донецька.pdf (accessed 24 September 2018).

25 See, for example, "Всеукраїнське муніципальне опитування", *Група Рейтинг*, 30 March 2016, http://ratinggroup.ua/research/regions/vseukrainskiy_municipalnyy_opros.html (accessed 24 September 2018).

26 See "Ринат Ахметов лидирует в рейтинге доверия украинцев на Донбассе", *Сегодня*, 9 June 2017, www.segodnya.ua/politics/rinat-ahmetov-lidiruet-v-reytinge-doveriya-ukraincev-opros-1028361.html (accessed 24 September 2018).

27 For details of this particular corruption scheme, see "Rotterdam+ Corruption Rents Counter", https://rotterdam.com.ua/ (accessed 24 September 2018).

5 From nomadic to entrenching occupation

Russian-sponsored state-building in Donbas

Given the nature of local identity in Donbas in spring 2014 – generally anti-Kyiv, but not necessarily pro-Moscow – and the highly fragmented state of politico-territorial 'organisation' in the rebel-controlled territories, Russia's aim of gaining full territorial and political control of Donbas, and thus the ability to either influence or destabilise any government in Kyiv, required the pursuit of three objectives: (1) physical removal from power of (actually or potentially) pro-Ukrainian social, political and economic elites in Donbas; and (2) deeper polarisation of society in Donbas in order to (3) facilitate mobilisation of hitherto marginalised groups from which to recruit local pro-Russian elites (Interviews 33, 45, 47, 48).

These objectives were highly interdependent in their realisation, and Russia faced significant challenges in achieving them. The main reason for this was that local society in Donetsk and Luhansk was generally characterised by a high level of internal cohesiveness, dense social networks, significant social capital, high level of public trust in local elites, and a well-developed regional identity (Mikheeva 2014).[1] Put differently, Donbas exhibited considerable potential for self-organisation, resilience and mobilisation in the face of Russia's intervention (UkrlifeTV 2017). However, in the simultaneously ensuing turf battles among the major political-economic groups in Ukraine, local and Kyiv-based Donbas elites were not given an opportunity to re-align with the new regime in Kyiv. They thus had few incentives to mobilise local resources in support of the government in Kyiv, but this did not automatically turn them into supporters of Russian-backed creeping occupation, especially as this posed a potentially considerable threat to their own interests (Interviews 50, 55, 56, 62).

In the following, we trace the evolution of the gradual de-fragmentation of the territory that now forms the DPR and LPR, beginning from late spring 2014 and the patchwork of highly localised power centres without any overarching framework of control to the more systematic and focused statebuilding efforts undertaken by Russia from the summer of 2014 onwards that established, in an institutional sense, the two people's republics as de-facto states on the territory of Ukraine.

Prelude: nomadic and creeping occupation to establish and extend territorial control in Donbas

The widely prevailing anarchy triggered by the anti-Maidan protests in Donbas led to the establishment of two other types politico-territorial arrangements in eastern Ukraine. The first of them was informally coor-dinated by local Ukrainian oligarchs who challenged the new government in Kyiv for control at the local level, seeking the maintenance of the local elite's political power and access to economic resources after the flight of Yanukovych. Local oligarchs, such as Rinat Akhmetov, used the remain-ing structures of Ukrainian local authorities, which continued operating until mid-November 2014, to keep their influence in the large industrially developed cities where they owned and/or controlled significant assets, including critical transport and communication infrastructure. This was the case, for example, in Donetsk and Yenakievo before Strelkov's occu-pation in July 2014 and in Mariupol before the Ukrainian army retook the city in May 2014. These local Ukrainian elites ('Donetskiye') were not interested in waging a real war against Kyiv, which would have resulted in the destruction of the very assets they were keen to control. Similar to Russian tactics at the time, but for very different reasons, these local elites encouraged and supported anti-Maidan protests in Donbas in order to strengthen their own negotiating position vis-à-vis the post-Maidan government in Kyiv (Interviews 10, 33).

In the city of Mariupol, for example, associates of Rinat Akhmetov took control in the wake of these anti-Maidan protests and began bargaining with Kyiv directly, while local authorities were more cautious and generally reluctant to challenge the central government in this way. This bargaining process accelerated as soon as Aleksander Boroday, the prime minister in the Russia-controlled wing of the DPR at the time, signalled his intention to expand territorial control towards Mariupol. Akhmetov and other Ukrainian Donetsk elites by quickly reaching an agreement with Kyiv, which allowed them to keep hold of their assets and the Ukrainian army, in the form of the paramilitary 'Azov' battalion, to restore full Ukrainian government control over Mariupol despite the fact local Ukrainian security forces were para-lysed.[2] These events in Mariupol illustrate some of the key dynamics in these early stages of the conflict, including the fluidity of alliances on the ground between various state and non-state actors (Kyiv, pro-Ukrainian paramilitaries, local elites) and their ability, at the time, to thwart the expan-sion of territorial control by Russian-backed forces.

The example of Mariupol is not an isolated case of how the intervention of private militias controlled by local oligarchs shaped the dynamics of the conflict in Donbas. Given the fluidity of the situation in the spring of 2014, elites from neighbouring oblasts of Donbas began to enter the fray, as well, in an attempt to take control of some of the spoils of the ongoing conflict. The city of Krasnoarmeysk (near the border between Donetsk and Dnipropetrovsk oblasts) also suffered from a power vacuum in March–May 2014. The city was partially controlled by Ukrainian police and partially by anti-Maidan paramilitary groups, with frequent clashes between them. On 11 May 2014 (the day of the referendum on independence in the DPR), the pro-governmental paramilitary battalion 'Dnepr' funded by Ukrainian oligarch Igor Kolomoysky (belonging to the 'Dnipropetrovskie' politico-economic group, which was in competition with the 'Donetskie' group) invaded Krasnoarmeysk and took power there. The 'Dnepr' battalion was camouflaged as an armoured escort of 'Privatbank' (a bank owned by Kolomoysky) in order to gain access to Krasnoarmeysk. Having entered the city, members of the battalion immediately occupied all important administrative buildings and forced out the anti-Maidan groups.[3] Shortly afterwards, troops of the National Guards of Ukraine entered the city. As a consequence of this 'private-public partnership,' Krasnoarmeysk remained outside the control of the DPR.

Yet, local elites competing over control of economic assets in post-Yanukovych Donbas were not the only local 'players,' and the multitude of other actors seriously complicated the situation and contributed to Kyiv's eventual loss of control over significant parts of the regions of Donetsk and Luhansk. The critical factor in this process was the collapse of Ukrainian institutions across Donbass which created opportunities for a pre-existing criminal sub-culture to flourish. For example, after the initial relative stabilisation in the DPR and LPR in 2014, the 'representatives' delegated by major local criminal clans occupied key positions in the economic structures of the government of the self-declared republics, such as Aleksandr Timofeev, who became minister of incomes and taxes in DPR.[4]

Small, economically and socially depressed cities built around coal-mining enterprises saw the rise of previously marginalised groups and organised criminals to capture local political power, often in cooperation with local security forces, or what remained of them after the flight of Yanukovych and the partial withdrawal of pro-Kyiv/pro-Ukrainian elites. Operating like warlords, local groups, led, for example, by local criminals-turned-warlords like Aleksandr Bednov, Pavel Dremov and Aleksey Mozgovoy, established a quasi-feudal system of rule in the territories they controlled relying on the extortion of local entrepreneurs, kidnapping, illegal extraction of resources, and the use of slave labour (Interviews 34, 44).[5] While the armed groups associated with these warlords did not participate in full-fledged battles against Ukrainian forces, they exhibited a much higher degree of violence against Ukrainian prisoners of war, pro-Ukrainian activists and civilians (International Partnership for Human Rights 2015). The system of rule that they established was, thus, significantly different from what was going on in areas controlled by Kremlin-sponsored groups under the control of people like Aleksander Zakharchenko and Igor Strelkov.

Thus, during the spring and early summer of 2014, three different types of politico-territorial arrangements emerged in eastern Ukraine that reflected different dimensions of the conflict locally and in relation to the new government in Kyiv and exhibited different degrees of Russian control and influence. This anarchical situation bore several risks for Russia and its strategy to use the conflict in eastern Ukraine as leverage over the government in Kyiv. First, there was a danger that an agreement might be achieved between the 'Donetskiye' and Kyiv that would facilitate the consensual return of Donbas under the Ukrainian government's control (as happened in one of Rinat Akhmetov's strongholds, Mariupol).[6] A second potential threat was declining local public support for any new arrangement and instead a popular preference to return to the status quo ante because of the lawlessness and criminality that the population of Donbas had to endure following the collapse of the Ukrainian state structures.[7]

Consequently, Russian destabilisation tactics escalated from nomadic to creeping occupation in order to consolidate territorial control in Donbas by rebel forces that were under the direct control of Moscow. The Kremlin's first objective, thus, was the physical removal from power of the local elite, including public servants, representatives of the middle class, liberal intellectuals, urban professionals and other local opinion leaders (International Federation for Human Rights and Center for Civil Liberties 2015). This was achieved through the use of instrumental violence, including widely publicised intimidation, torture and executions of local leaders (International Partnership for Human Rights 2015). This resulted in the intended exodus that critically undermined society's will and ability to resist Russian control (Interviews 45, 48, Workshops B, C, K).

Russia's second objective was to deepen social polarisation along ethnic lines and between different social strata in Donbas, which was considered a prerequisite for achieving its third objective, namely to mobilise hitherto marginalised groups as a support base for, and recruitment pool of, new local pro-Russian elites that could eventually take over from Russian and Transnistrian 'imports,' thus allowing Russia to maintain the fiction of its non-involvement while simultaneously ensuring a higher level of control over Donbas elites than it had during the initial period of nomadic occupation (Workshop E, Workshop G). Capitalising on pre-existing distrust towards the pro-Western elites in Kyiv and a significant degree of political exclusion and economic deprivation, Russia was able to create a perception of upward social mobility under a new regime for those who lacked any such prospects under successive Kyiv governments (Interviews 46, 47, Workshop L). Empowering socially excluded groups in an ideational sense by giving them a future perspective and in a material sense by providing them with the means and at times leadership to pursue such promising new perspectives (Workshops D, F), in turn, also created the manpower necessary to achieve the first objective, the physical removal from power of local elites. Hence, a pool of willing 'executioners' became readily available to escalate conflict locally, displace local elites and prepare the ground for their replacement.[8]

The events in Donetsk in July 2014 illustrate this process of how Russia took control through various proxies in this period of creeping occupation. As soon as the so-called Russian Orthodox Army (*slavyantsi*) of about 3,000 troops occupied the city of Donetsk on 5 July 2014, Boroday and Strelkov, who had earlier appointed themselves as prime minister and minister of defence of the DPR, respectively, co-opted local militia leaders Aleksander Zakharchenko, commander of the 'Oplot' battalion, and Aleksander Khodakovsky, commander of the 'Vostok' battalion, as head of the security service of the DPR and as military commander of Donetsk, respectively. The new military-political leadership of the DPR was then further strengthened by experienced operatives from Transnistria, including Vladimir Antyufeev, the former head of the Transnistrian state security services, who was appointed deputy head of the Cabinet of Ministers with responsibility for law enforcement, while his former colleagues Oleg Bereza and Andrey Pinchuk, respectively, occupied the positions of minister of internal affairs and state security of the DPR. As a result of the changes in leadership, the *varangians*[9] from Russia and Transnistria composed the core of political and military command of DPR in this most critical period for the survival of the DPR in what was at the time an intense military conflict with the Ukrainian army.

The influx of operatives from Transnistria was part of Russia's earliest attempts at state-building in Donbas, partially reversing some of the damage done in the immediate aftermath of the pro-Russian takeover of Donetsk. As Pinchuk (2017, 45) notes. The DPR did not have the capacity to establish its own administrative bodies. It did not have any resources of its own. The appointment of 'people's delegates' to important position in the government resulted in the full paralysis of decision-making . . . Strelkov who pushed out the Ukrainian mayor and other authorities from Donetsk, put the city on the verge of collapse.

From a different perspective, this is confirmed by the Ukrainian mayor of Donetsk at the time, Oleksander Lukyanchenko, who was forced out by Igor Strelkov:

> the DPR did not have the capacity to establish its own administrative bodies. It did not have any resources of its own. The appointment of

'people's delegates' to important position in the government resulted in the full paralysis of decision-making. . . . Strelkov who pushed out the Ukrainian mayor and other authorities from Donetsk, put the city on the verge of . . . the DPR demanded from me to organize the supplies for DPR troops instead of civilians. . . . They told me that they [the military] are not interested in civilians and civilian life in the city.[10]

One of the perverse, although not entirely unexpected, consequences of Russia's more assertive takeover of rebel-controlled areas of Donbas was the replication of the very oligarchic institutions that at least some of the early rebels had sought to do away with. Despite the physical removal of the entire strata of the former local elites from Donbas, the institutions of the oligarchic state were reproduced, albeit in Russia's image, as Igor Strelkov, the former minister of defence of the DPR, explained:

> there is no people's power in Donetsk and Luhansk. They are copying the Russian oligarchic system . . . sometimes in a very ridiculous way . . . Donetsk was blooming before the war, now it is in a chaos.[11]

Roman Manekin, an ex-minister in the DPR administration, subsequently arrested there and now living in Moscow, echoes this sentiment in a more detailed way:

> Donbas-Malorossia is a never-ending civil war, a zone of instability in Ukraine with the fireplace in Donetsk . . . gangsterism as a method of public governance, the absence of political freedoms and parties, warlordism, dependence of population on humanitarian aid, thefts, nepotism, corruption, poverty of population and shameless demonstration of power by the new Donetsk elite.[12]

Yet, the Russian-Transnistrian period in July and August 2014 proved to be, from the perspective of the personnel involved, a relatively brief, albeit impactful, interregnum. As soon as a degree of order and control had been established alongside basic institutions and minimal public services, Moscow initiated an exchange of elites, partly in an attempt to 'localise' the leaderships of the nascent DPR and LPR. As Aleksandr Boroday explained:

> before August 2014, I was the prime-minister of DPR. In August 2014, I needed to go. The Minsk process was evolving. . . . The government of 'Free Donbas' looked very comical: I was a resident of Moscow. My deputy-prime minister Vladimir Antyufeev was a Russian citizen as well. All *siloviki* were either Russian citizens or from Transnistria. In

order to speak on behalf of DPR and LPR in Minsk, we needed to find someone from the Donbas region.[13]

Thus, when, by late August 2014, the fighting reached a stalemate on the ground with newly elected Ukrainian President Petro Poroshenko unable to make decisive territorial gains or inflict significant losses on the increasingly well-organised and equipped forces of the two self-proclaimed people's republics of Donetsk and Luhansk and their institutionally better performing *hinterland*, Russia and its proxies in Donbas were well prepared for negotiations. Under military pressure, Kyiv agreed to a further round of negotiations in the Belarusian capital of Minsk, which resulted in the first of two Minsk Agreements on 5 September 2014, followed by an additional protocol two weeks later. Yet again, implementation was at best selective and eventually stalled completely.

Entrenching occupation and beyond: the intensification of state-building efforts

Subsequent parliamentary elections in Ukraine in October saw a strong showing of the pro-Western, anti-Russian bloc, but also exposed deep divisions and a high degree of apathy among the population with a national turnout of just over half of eligible voters, and less than a third in Kyiv-controlled areas of Donetsk and Luhansk regions. Yet, the election results were arguably a trigger for Moscow to capitalise on the successful deployment of its earlier destabilisation tactics during the periods of nomadic and creeping occupation. Realising that no pro-Russian regime in Kyiv was likely to emerge in the near future, Russia shifted its approach from the managed destabilisation tactics of nomadic and creeping occupation – which were focused on undermining Ukrainian efforts at consolidating the country's post-Maidan Western trajectory by creating a sufficient level of (violent) instability in Donbas – to an approach that pursued the institutional strengthening of the separatist regions and to build them up into capable pro-Russian players in an otherwise hostile, pro-Western Ukraine (Workshop G, Workshop K). With the conditions for 'state-building' put in place due to the success of societal destabilisation in Donbas prior to the autumn of 2014, and with a partially positive track record of an earlier, albeit much more rudimentary, Russian-sponsored and Russian-led state-building effort, the Russian-backed republican governments in Donetsk and Luhansk embarked on a much more comprehensive path to state-building, including the reorganisation of uncoordinated forces into a 'regular' army and police under centralised command, the delivery of public services by the republican authorities and closer integration into the Russian economic and legal space (Interviews 28, 29, 37).[14]

A conduit of this new phase of entrenching occupation was the gradually escalating violence on the ground: as a resolution of the crisis on Russian terms became more and more unlikely, and as Moscow continued to establish a 'proper' de-facto state within the recognised international borders of Ukraine, the actual extent of Russian-controlled territory and its military and infrastructural viability acquired higher priority for both sides, but simultaneously led to intensified efforts in the so-called Normandy format to rescue the first Minsk agreement and its implementation protocol. These talks continued on and off throughout January and early February, but it was not before a sixteen-hour negotiation marathon on 11–12 February among the four countries' leaders that the second Minsk agreement was concluded, almost a year to the date after the 2014 Kyiv Agreement. Unsurprisingly, some initial optimism on the sustainability of this agreement quickly evaporated – fighting continued around the strategic railway intersection of Debaltsevo, with both sides taking heavy losses and the Russia-backed rebels eventually capturing the town a week after Minsk II. Again, the agreement was implemented selectively and slowly – enough to avoid, so far, a return to all-out war, but nowhere comprehensively enough to demonstrate either side's commitment to a peaceful settlement of the conflict (Interviews 14, 19, 22, Workshops I, J).

The consolidation of territorial gains, and their entrenchment through the two Minsk agreements in September 2014 and February 2015, put the rebels and their backers in Moscow firmly in control in the DPR and LPR, and simultaneously required them to assume the responsibilities that this situation created vis-à-vis the civilian population. In other words, further concerted efforts at state-building were required. These gathered pace from late 2014 onwards, and took several forms.

As a first step to create a minimum of legitimacy for the republican leaderships and to restore some degree of order and predictability in governance, presidential and parliamentary elections took place simultaneously in Donetsk and Luhansk on 2 November 2014. Despite the fact that turnout was minimal (not least given the large number of IDPs and refugees), that there were no independent media to support candidates other than the two eventually elected, that Ukrainian candidates and parties were banned, and that not even Moscow recognised the elections formally, the elections laid the ground for the establishment of a better function political regime in the DPR and LPR. Not only did the two presidents elected, the late Aleksander Zakharchenko and Leonid Plotnitsky, represent the self-declared republics in all subsequent negotiations, but state-building has since also been based on a semblance of legislative processes in the parliaments of the DPR and LPR. While this is not to suggest that this is in any way indicative of a democratic process, it nonetheless marks an improvement compared to the situation prior to November 2014. Until then, any kind of legislation was absent. As noted earlier, different politico-territorial entities operated different regimes, subject to which configuration of warlords, local criminals, and/or Russian mercenaries had effective control (Interviews 57, 62).

By way of illustration, within the first year of its existence, the newly elected parliament of DPR has adopted about 20 laws regulating security and military affairs, the majority of which was adopted in the period between November 2014 and February 2015. In addition, there have been 42 laws regulating the socio-economic and cultural affairs (the majority adopted in summer and autumn 2015), and 24 laws regulating administrative and legal affairs (most of them adopted between autumn 2015 and winter 2016). This demonstrates the early focus on military and security affairs that established the framework for the republican armed forces, the police, the prosecutor's office, and the border protection forces. In parallel with legislative efforts, the rebel authorities moved to establish, in a Weberian sense, their monopoly on the use of force in the occupied territories. Building on earlier, more rudimentary attempts to centralise power and forge a unified command and control structure across various armed units, the republican authorities took decisive steps against the remaining warlords who still resisted centralisation: Aleksandr Bednov (a.k.a. Betman) was killed by special forces of the LPR on 1 January 2015; Aleksey Mozgovoy, commander of the LPR's 'Prizrak' battalion, was assassinated by an unknown person on 23 May 2015; Pavel Dremov, commander of the LPR's Cossack guard, died in a bomb attack on the day of his wedding on 12 December 2015; Arsen Pavlov, a.k.a. Motorola, commander of the DPR's Somali battalion, was killed in a bomb attack in the lift of his house on 16 October 2016; Mikhail Tolstikh, a.k.a. Givi, a colonel in the DPR forces, died in an arson attack in this office on 8 February 2017; and most recently the DPR 'head of state' Alexander Zakharchenko was killed in a bomb attack in Donetsk on 31 August 2018.

In stark contrast, legislative efforts in relation to socio-economic and cultural policy were almost completely absent until the spring of 2015. Since May that year, along with the start of centralised payment of pensions and salaries to public sector employees from the republican budget, Donetsk and Luhansk adopted fiscal legislation and established fiscal bodies, collecting taxes from local business (Interviews 50, 51, 52). Private firms operating in both DPR and LPR, and Ukraine, found themselves exposed to double taxation: businesses paid taxes to both Ukrainian and republican budgets, including a special 'military tax,' supporting the sides' opposing armed forces. At the same time, the main industries located in rebel-controlled territories have faced a lack of investment from Russia and Ukraine, while local and foreign owners have frequently suspended production, partly also because of the disruption to the banking, communication and transport infrastructure that followed Ukraine's decision to pursue a policy of isolation of the DPR and LPR from November 2014 onwards (Interviews 22, 23).

The direct impact of the armed conflict on business, of course, goes beyond Ukraine's isolation policy. The physical destruction of infrastructure in the course of hostilities was very significant. Large areas along the border between the Ukraine-controlled and rebel-controlled territories (cities, villages and agricultural fields) have been mined and there has been a significant build-up in military fortifications accommodating about fifty thousand Ukrainian and forty thousand rebel troops. Furthermore, the internal displacement of around 1.6 million people in Ukraine and an additional roughly one million refugees in Russia,[15] as well as significant levels of emigration among professionals and skilled workers, have gradually deprived local businesses of the necessary workforce to sustain their operations. This near-complete collapse of the economy in the war-affected territories of Donbas, thus, led to somewhere between 1.1 million and 1.8 million lost jobs, equivalent to about 50% of the nominal labour force at large-scale enterprises and 90% at small-sized and medium-sized enterprises in both government-controlled and rebel-controlled parts of Donbas. While part of this surge in unemployment was 'compensated' by war-related migratory flows, it still had a massive impact on the socio-economic structure of the DPR and LPR, creating a situation in which pensions, salaries and other subsidies (in large part paid for by Russia) for socially vulnerable groups, army, police, local authorities, and a wide range of public employees in the education, healthcare, culture and municipal infrastructure sectors is the main source of income for the population in the de-facto entities (Interviews 40, 51).

The political system that emerged in the two entities is characterised not only by a high degree of centralisation of power, but also by its personalisation. The president of each republic is simultaneously the head of the executive branch and commander-in-chief, while the parliaments are too weak, constitutionally and in practice, to offer any real balance to check presidential power.[16] This makes for both an effective decision-making process and one that can be more directly controlled by Moscow without any threats from more independent lawmakers. Given that republican authorities in both the DPR and LPR, and their backers in Moscow, are now almost wholly responsible for the provision of public goods and services following the imposition of an economic and transport blockade by Kyiv against the DPR and LPR, the incremental yet steady improvement in living conditions (restoration of law and order, public services, etc.) has contributed to an increase in the internal legitimacy of the regimes in the DPR and LPR, despite the fact that significant limitations on human rights and fundamental freedoms of the local population have remained in place (Interviews 51, 56). With ministries and other public bodies of the republics directly subordinate to the respective ministries in Moscow, the character of the political regimes in Donetsk and Luhansk is, again, deeply clientelist with its structures built and sustained around the (re-)distribution of Russian financial aid.

The republican authorities' state-building efforts were additionally complicated by two factors. As we noted earlier, there is a large transient population that regularly crosses the front line and has connections on both sides without developing clear loyalties. Thus, even those who are formally residents of the self-declared republics have retained their Ukrainian citizenship and continue to rely on the Ukrainian system of justice, education, healthcare and social security. Even though Russia now recognises the passports issued by the DPR and LPR, it continues to require Ukrainian passports for any financial activities or legal proceedings, thus treating their residents as citizens of Ukraine. This poses clear limits as to how far *state*-building can go.

Closely related to the citizenship question is, for the time being at least, a Russian strategy to keep open the possibility of the reintegration of the DPR and LPR into Ukraine under the terms of Minsk II, i.e., serving as a base inside Ukraine from which to promote the 'Russian vector' of Ukraine's foreign policy. Even though there is no immediate likelihood of such reintegration happening (not least because of Kyiv's rejection of such a threat to the country's fragile political sovereignty), the longer-term uncertainty that possible, if not probable, reintegration implies favours rent-seeking behaviour among the new republican elites (from smuggling, trade in arms, drugs, natural resources and other illegal business activities) and has resulted in further changes to the demographic structure of the population towards its aged segments, with high levels of emigration of the able-bodied, working-age population and students from the DPR and LPR.[17] The decline of the productive workforce and the dependency of those remaining behind on the public purse put additional question marks on the longer-term economic viability of the state-building project in these two de-facto entities, not least also in light over uncertainty as to how long Russia will be able and willing to subsidise the republics (Interviews 35, 36, 57).

This uncertainty, therefore, poses a major problem also in terms of *identity*-building. However, the notion of uncertainty, in one reading of Russian policy, represents rather wishful thinking. As Igor Strelkov put it:

> For four years of war in Donbas, its disease has been progressing. The root of this disease is uncertainty of Donbas's future. For four years,

Donbas has been pushed into Ukraine with some conditions. Ukraine does not agree. There is ongoing war, the borders are closed. . . . Unlike Abkhazia and Ossetia, Russian citizenship for residents of DPR and LPR is not an option either. There are custom barriers between Russia and the republics. . . . This policy supplements consistent talks of Russian officials that Donbas has to return to Ukraine.[18]

While Strelkov, too, proclaims uncertainty as a major problem, his own assessment points to rather less uncertainty, given that Russian policy appears to close off specific scenarios by favouring reintegration of Donbas into Ukraine not only rhetorically but also by means of a number of practical steps, like customs barriers and the denial of Russian citizenship. We will return to the issue of future scenarios in the following chapter, but it is worthwhile pointing out that Russian policy vis-à-vis Transnistria and the two de-facto states of Abkhazia and South Ossetia has displayed many similar features. A rhetorical and practical Russian commitment to reintegration still prevails in the context of Transnistria, and it did so in the case of Abkhazia and South Ossetia until just before the 2008 war, while 'passportisation' was not a feature in either of these conflicts in their early days.[19]

With several 'alternatives' to uncertainty thus unavailable, at least for the foreseeable future, the question of local citizenship is critically important for the consolidation of the self-declared republics and the strengthening of their internal and external legitimacy. With the exception of the unrecognised referenda on independence in May 2014 and the equally unrecognised elections in November 2014, the residents of Donetsk and Luhansk have not been given a choice regarding their citizenship since 1991. Legally, the residents of the rebel-controlled territories remain citizens of Ukraine. However, they are also considered as 'citizens' of DPR or LPR by the republican authorities.[20] Since 2014, Russia partially recognised documents issued by the authorities of the self-declared republics. However, important legal procedures – such as on migration, property rights, financial operations and civic status – remain inaccessible for holders of DPR/LPR passports.

The isolation that residents of the DPR and LPR thus face on both sides (i.e., Russia and Ukraine) is further compounded by equivalent policies in the self-declared republics that restrict travel to Ukraine-controlled territory. By way of illustration, on 15 December 2017, the DPR's then 'head of state,' the late Aleksander Zakharchenko, signed a decree which forbids travel to Ukraine for certain groups of population: 'public servants,' employees of organisations funded from the republican budget (education, healthcare, culture, local administration, public transport and others) and employees of the captured industrial enterprises.[21] For the self-declared republics, this 'freezing' of relations with Kyiv promises more secure institutions, a more stable economy and a more predictable population size. Not dissimilar to the building of the Berlin Wall by the East German regime in 1961, such expected benefits are conceivable in the short term, but doubtful in the long term. Similarly, this degree of external and self-isolation is unprecedented in the post-Soviet context. Transnistria is economically well-integrated with Moldova, Russia and the EU, and people-to-people contacts across the ceasefire line remain by and large unproblematic. In the context of Abkhazia and South Ossetia the picture is different with regard to links with Georgia and the EU, but both entities are far more integrated with Russia than the DPR and LPR.

Thus, the uncertainty about the future of the two entities in Donbas is as much one rooted in a lack of clarity of their trajectory as it is one of a lack of an obvious precedent. However, as we discuss in the next chapter, this has not stopped analysts and policy makers from considering the feasibility of, and in fact promote, various scenarios for the settlement of the underlying conflict.

Notes

1 These findings were also confirmed separately by another of our interlocutors (Interview 19).
2 "Корбан: Ахметов решил поторговаться с Киевом, чтобы сохранить влияние на Донбассе, но переблефовал и сейчас страдает", Interview with Gennady Korban, 23 October 2015, http://gordonua.com/publications/korban-ahmetov-reshil-potorgovatsya-s-kievom-chtoby-sohranit-vliyanie-na-don-basse-no-pereblefoval-i-seychas-stradaet-103299.html (accessed 24 September 2018).
3 The events were partially captured in a report by vesti.ru. While clearly not without bias in its reporting and use of emotive language, the coverage still offers a glimpse at the prevailing chaos during this phase of the conflict. See "Бойня в Красноармейске: мирных жителей расстреливал каратель-снайпер", 13 May 2014, www.vesti.ru/doc.html?id=1574590&tid=105474 (accessed 24 September 2018).
4 See "Журналист рассказал о конфликте Захарченко с 'главным рейдером' ДНР", https://apostrophe.ua/news/society/accidents/2016-05-14/jurnalist-rasskazal-o-konflikte-zaharchenko-s-glavnyim-reyderom-dnr/58936 (accessed 24 September 2018).
5 See for example, "ЗВІТ ПРО ОЦІНКУ СТАНОВИЩА. РОМІВ В УКРАЇНІ ТА ВПЛИВУ ПОТОЧНОЇ КРИЗИ", www.osce.org/uk/odihr/131776?download=true (accessed 24 September 2018); "Доповідь щодо ситуації з правами людини в Україні", 16 листопада 2016 р.–15 лютого 2017, www.ohchr.org/Documents/Countries/UA/UAReport17th_UKR.pdf (accessed 24 September 2018); "КОАЛІЦІЯ ПРЕЗЕНТУВАЛА РЕЗУЛЬТАТИ МОНІТОРИНГУ ПОРУШЕНЬ ПРАВ ЛЮДИНИ НА ДОНБАСІ НА КОНФЕРЕНЦІЇ ОБСЄ З ПРАВ ЛЮДИНИ", https://jfp.org.ua/coalition/novyny-koalicii/articles/osce-hdim (accessed 24 September 2018).

6 Consequently, as noted earlier, Akhmetov's economic and humanitarian networks and structures were forced out of the rebel-controlled parts of Donbas.
7 A particularly notorious example of this was the case of Vadym Pogodin, the commander of the 'Kertch' battalion of the DPR. He is alleged to have killed a local teenager for expressing pro-Ukrainian sympathies in July 2014 in rebel-controlled Donetsk (Interviews 27, 44). See also "Выбили зубы, потом – пять выстрелов в голову", 27 July 2017, www.novayagazeta.ru/ articles/2017/07/28/73261-rasstrel (accessed 24 September 2018).
8 An illustrative example of this is the 'Sparta' battalion of the rebels in Donetsk. Led by Russian mercenary Arsen Pavlov (aka 'Motorola'), himself a veteran of several Russian military campaigns who failed to reintegrate into civilian life in Russia, members of 'Sparta' are infamous for their cruelty against Ukrainian troops on the battlefield and in captivity (Interview 39). See also Mikheeva (2015).
9 Historically, 'varangians' were leaders of Scandinavian tribes which were invited to establish and govern what became the Kievan Rus' in the late 9th century. Since then, the term 'varangians' refers to externally appointed rulers or administrators.
10 "Донецк остался без мэра, горожане ждут худшего", Interview with Oleksander Lukyanchenko, 15 July 2014, РИА Новости Украина, http://rian.com. ua/story/20140715/354896463.html (accessed 24 September 2018).
11 "Исполнит ли Стрелков приказ Путина? Киев тоже будет нашим! Интервью НОД с Игорем Стрелковым", 26 February 2016, www.youtube. com/watch?v=hbhQLsDTedU (accessed 24 September 2018).
12 See https://my.mail.ru/mail/manekin.65/multipost/141400003B825002.html. Post dated 19 July 2017 at 22:55 (accessed 2 November 2018).
13 "В гостях у Захара Прилепина Александр Бородай", www.youtube. com/watch?v=rPq5J-Xt2o8&list=PLoakhgttSsPoE9VwoCu-MdZF4FU7-GswR&index=26 (accessed 24 September 2018).
14 See also OTR Online (2017) and Gushchin et al. (2016).
15 According to data from Ukrainian statistical agencies, about 3.0–3.5 million people live in the rebel-controlled territories, including 500,000 children and 900,000 pensioners. About 1.6 million people have registered as IDPs in Ukraine, including about 350,000 based in Ukraine-controlled territories in Donbas. A further 353,000 former residents of the rebel-controlled territories received refugee status in Russia and Belarus, while 570,000 live there due to other reasons (primarily as labour migrants). However, it is difficult to assess the real number of people residing in rebel-controlled areas because a significant part of the population of Donbas migrates regularly across and/or is simultaneously registered as IDPs in Ukraine and/or refugees in Russia (or Belarus), but in reality has the rebel-controlled areas of Donetsk or Luhansk as their main place of residence. At the same time, there is clear tendency of IDPs from Ukraine returning to their former homes in the DPR and LPR, which results from discrimination and stigmatisation of IDPs from Donbas in Ukraine, insufficient state support of IDPs and limited opportunities to find employment, and the deepening and radicalization of anti-Russian attitudes manifested by right-wing nationalist movements targeting IDPs from the DPR and LPR.
16 See Конституция Донецкой Народной Республики, available at https:// dnr-online.ru/download/konstitutsiya-donetskoj-narodnoj-respubliki/ and

Конституция Луганской Народной Республики, availabe at https://nslnr.su/
zakonodatelstvo/normativno-pravovaya-baza/591/ for the constitutions of the
DPR and LNR, respectively (accessed 24 September 2018).

17 "Щодо надання послуг службою зайнятості внутрішньо переміщеним
особам за період з 1 березня 2014 року по 31 серпня 2017 року", www.dcz.
gov.ua/statdatacatalog/document?id=351058 (accessed 24 September 2018).

18 See "Игорь Стрелков: вооруженный конфликт между Украиной и Россией
неизбежен", 23 June 2018, https://vk.com/video347260249_456239236?list=d
d4069bbbd2ab95ac6 (accessed 24 September 2018).

19 Passportisation in these cases did not really become a major Russian foreign
policy instrument until the early 2000s. While the policy has extended Russian citizenship to upwards of 90% of Abkhazia's residents and almost 100% of
South Ossetia's, figures for Transnistria are much lower, given that only around
30% of residents there are ethnic Russians, with roughly the same number of
ethnic Ukrainians and ethnic Moldovans. Moreover, Donbas is also of a completely different demographic scale which imposes limits at least on the speed of
any similarly complete passportisation: the combined estimated population of
the DPR and LPR is between 3.0 and 3.5 million, i.e., approximately four times
that of the around 55,000 residents of South Ossetia, 250,000 of Abkhazia and
less than 500,000 of Transnistria. On Russian passportisation in the latter three
cases, see Nagashima (2017).

20 For example, the so-called Declaration of Citizenship adopted by the 'parliament' of the self-declared Luhansk People's Republic considers all citizens of
Ukraine who were formally registered on the rebel-controlled territories on the
date of the 'referendum on independence of LPR' as 'citizens' of LPR.

21 "Государственным служащим временно запрещен выезд на территорию
Украины", https://dnr-online.ru/gossluzhashhim-vremenno-zapreshhen-vyezd-
na-territoriyu-ukrainy/ (accessed 24 September 2018).

6 From conflict management to conflict settlement

The interplay of domestic and external factors

As one of our interlocutors (Interview 38) put it, "Russia's strategic goal is to maintain control over its Near Abroad. The methods to do so may change over time, but the goal itself can and will not be changed." If this is the approach taken by Moscow, and there is little to suggest that this is not the case, then it offers a useful lens through which to interpret the existing four agreements – the Kyiv of Agreement of February 2014, the Geneva Agreement of April 2014 and the two Minsk Agreements of September 2014 and February 2015 – and assess the feasibility and viability of various scenarios put forward for an eventual settlement of the conflict in eastern Ukraine.

Thus, we proceed in two steps. First, we summarise the provisions in each agreement and argue that they represent an increasingly pro-Russian set of provisions extending the degree to which Russia would have been able to exert influence in Ukraine had any of these agreements been fully implemented. The four agreements are thus the reference points that we use to trace relevant developments, respectively, in the periods before, between and after them to illustrate the evolution of the conflict. The periods preceding and following each of the four political agreements were characterised by distinct developments on the ground in Donbas that went hand in hand with a gradual escalation of Russian destabilisation policies against Ukraine and, arguably, insufficient pushback from Ukraine's Western partners.

Building on the analysis in the preceding chapters, we argue that each failed agreement implementation went hand in hand with an escalation of destabilisation efforts. In the period between late February and mid-April 2014, Russia supported and funded anti-Maidan protests in mainland eastern Ukraine.[1] From mid-April 2014, Russia began supporting the rebels initially with money and weapons. This was the period of 'nomadic' occupation. As a Ukrainian offensive gained momentum and territory in early summer 2014, Russia strengthened the rebels first through supplying more and more equipment, including heavier weapons, advisers and eventually through a clandestine invasion of 'vacationers' in mid-August. This led to a period of 'creeping' occupation by the rebels, who began to regain territory they had lost in May and June. As a result, by August 2014, fighting had significantly intensified from the usage of small arms in the early clashes of April 2014 to using tanks, heavy artillery and multiple rocket systems, aircraft and anti-aircraft defence systems (Interview 23).[2] This major escalation of fighting and the losses suffered by the Ukrainian side facilitated a return to negotiations, producing the first Minsk Agreement on 5 September 2014. An immediate failure of this agreement was averted by an additional protocol two weeks later, but eventually the volatile ceasefire established broke down and fighting resumed. Following the parliamentary elections in Ukraine on 26 October 2014 with the strong performance of pro-Western, anti-Russian forces, any prospects of a pro-Russian government had clearly evaporated, and Russia now began to focus on consolidating the rebels' territorial gains. Thus, the period of 'entrenching' occupation began, accompanied by more pronounced and comprehensive efforts at state-building in Donbas. A simultaneous escalation of fighting to create militarily and strategically more viable rebel territories pressured Ukraine into another round of negotiations, which produced the second Minsk agreement. Following the rebel capture of Debaltsevo, a more or less stable line of control was established between the Sides that has remained in place despite sporadic clashes and very little progress on the implementation of the political provisions of Minsk II (Interviews 14, 21, 29), indicating that, despite its volatility, the two sides have settled, at least temporarily, for the existing status quo.[3]

Thus, this first section of this chapter offers a more detailed analytical narrative that elaborates and traces the blended nature of this conflict in relation to the antagonistic penetration of the post-Soviet region in which it has evolved since late 2013, emphasising the connections between the dynamics on the local, national and regional/global levels of analysis.

In a second step, we then use this analysis as a reference point against which we examine three prominent settlement scenarios – the Croatian, German and Transnistrian scenarios, respectively – and consider two further scenarios of our own – the Crimean and the Georgian scenarios. This is not meant to make a normative or pragmatic case for accommodating Russian demands, but rather to acknowledge that there is a Russian position that needs to be taken into account when considering the feasibility of any possible settlement and to examine conflict management alternatives (as opposed to conflict settlement) and their implications.

Four agreements, no settlement: the pathway towards new de-facto states in eastern Ukraine

The purpose of the following section is to establish, by way of a textual analysis, why each of the agreements negotiated so far for the conflict failed to gain traction towards full implementation and, in turn, led to an increasingly ever more hard-line approach by Russia to securing its influence in Ukraine in the very terms of each subsequent agreement.

The Kyiv agreement was concluded on 21 February 2014 between then Ukrainian president, Viktor Yanukovych and three leaders of the parliamentary opposition – Vitaliy Klichko, Oleh Tyahnibok and Arsenij Yatseniuk – witnessed by foreign ministers of France, Poland and Germany.[4] Although a special envoy of the Russian president had also participated in the negotiations, he did not sign the agreement as a witness. The agreement establishes a period of transition until the end of 2014, encompassing a government of national unity formed by the signatory parties, constitutional reform aimed at a better balance of powers between parliament and president, and presidential elections following the adoption of a new constitution. This would have provided for a managed transition during which Russia's main ally at the time, President Yanukovych, would have shared power with the parliamentary opposition. The outcome of the transition, however, would have been open-ended in terms of both the constitutional nature of Ukraine and its next president. Russia's limited enthusiasm for the agreement is, thus, not difficult to understand, but in the actual course of events, the fatal blow was dealt by the extra-parliamentary Euromaidan opposition who rejected the agreement. Having also lost the support of his own power base,[5] Yanukovych found himself in an unsustainable situation and fled to Russia.

This clearly represented a significant problem for Moscow, as it was then left without a major source of influence in Kyiv and with no clear pathway to regain any, either, as the timeline initially envisaged would have kept open a path for Moscow to have at least some indirect influence over Ukrainian politics through securing favourable terms in a constitutional reform process whose conduct and outcome would have seen the participation of pro-Russian forces. A statement by the Russian foreign ministry consequently noted:

> [w]e are surprised that several European politicians have already sprung to support the announcement of presidential elections in Ukraine this May, although the agreement of the 21 February envisages that these elections should take place only after the completion of the constitutional reform. It is clear that for this reform to succeed all the Ukrainian

political forces and all regions of the country must become its part, but its results should be approved by a nationwide referendum.[6]

The policy escalation that followed (see ahead) in the period after the collapse of the Kyiv agreement paved the way to the next agreement, the so-called Geneva Statement on Ukraine released by the US, EU, Ukraine and Russia on 17 April 2014.[7] While vague in some respects, the Statement establishes a disarmament process and a broad amnesty, as well as, for the purposes of constitutional reform, "a broad national dialogue, with outreach to all of Ukraine's regions and political constituencies, and allow for the consideration of public comments and proposed amendments." This latter provision constitutes a specification of the constitutional reform process not present in the Kyiv Agreement of February 2014, and arguably creates an additional opportunity for the representation of pro-Russian interests within it by specifically mentioning "regions and constituencies" and making reference to a "national dialogue." The latter is also a recurrent theme in official statements when it comes to Russia pushing for direct negotiations between the government in Kyiv and the de-facto authorities in Donbas. A statement by the Russian foreign ministry on 13 April, for example, emphasises the need to "immediately start a true, national dialogue with equal participation of all the regions in the interests of the organisation of swift and radical constitutional reform,"[8] while references later abound drawing parallels to national dialogue processes elsewhere, such as in Afghanistan, Libya, Iraq, Yemen, Mali and South Sudan, and argue that in Ukraine, too, the government should directly engage with opposition forces in Donbas.[9]

Similarly, the endorsement of a leading role for the OSCE Special Monitoring Mission and the committing of US, EU and Russian monitors ensures a continuing 'legal' Russian foothold in the crisis in Ukraine, while paving the way towards an internationalised monitoring, and thus stabilisation and entrenchment, of an emerging boundary line within Ukraine. Through the constraints that this placed on Ukraine's sovereignty, alongside with the disarmament requirements on "all illegal armed groups" (thus including Ukrainian 'volunteers' who had borne the brunt of the fighting until then), Russia laid the foundations for a potentially emerging de-facto state in Donbas before this appeared as a seriously pursued option in the next stage of the conflict. With likely the same objective in mind, Russia kept pushing for some official status for representatives from Donbas, with Russian Foreign Minister Sergey Lavrov noting at his press conference immediately after the conclusion of the Geneva talks in April 2014 that it was necessary to secure "the immediate establishment of a broad national dialogue within the framework of the constitutional process, which should be inclusive, transparent and accountable, is required" and that the talks had "emphasised that all the Ukrainian regions and political forces should be involved into this dialogue."[10] Having 'learned' from the failure of the Kyiv agreement, Russia at least partially hedged against a similar fate with the Geneva Statement, bringing in the OSCE as an implementer, and thus implicitly an international guarantor, of the agreement, while further working towards securing a status for representatives from Donbas and the 'region' itself.

With militias in the Donbas region refusing to disarm and to end their occupation of government facilities, there was no progress on constitutional reform, and the activities of the OSCE mission became the only element of real implementation. However, an attempt by the OSCE to have a roadmap for the implementation of the Geneva Declaration agreed initially failed (even though the Geneva Declaration was re-confirmed in the Normandy format in early July 2014).[11] Worse still, fighting soon escalated – in the form of Ukraine's so-called anti-terrorist operation and the increasingly muscular Russian response to it (see ahead).

This triggered a renewed international effort towards a settlement resulting in the first Minsk Agreement of 5 September 2015, concluded under the auspices of the so-called Trilateral Contact Group consisting of representatives of the OSCE, Russia, Ukraine and, notably, the separatists. The marked qualitative change in Minsk I, compared to previous agreements, is the specific stipulation to "[i]mplement decentralization of power, including by means of enacting the Law of Ukraine 'With respect to the temporary status of local self-government in certain areas of the Donetsk and the Lugansk regions' (Law on Special Status)." and to "ensure the holding of early local elections" in accordance with this law.[12] If implemented, this so-called temporary status of the separatist-controlled areas and the political legitimation of separatist leaders through local elections would have fundamentally altered the situation in Ukraine and established a de-facto state, albeit with yet unspecified local powers and influence at the centre. This was again an indication of an approach aimed at strengthening the representation of pro-Russian interests, including in the "inclusive national dialogue" that the agreement reiterates. This long-standing Russian determination to have the de-facto authorities in Donbas accepted as direct negotiation partners also becomes apparent when the Russian foreign minister points out that although originally established in the Geneva agreement, "a national dialogue immediately with participation of all the Ukrainian regions" only began in September when "it [was] possible to convince the Ukrainian leadership to sit at the negotiation table with the militia."[13] In fact, a month later, Lavrov goes as far as confirming some success in the Russian strategy of both building a de-facto state and legitimising its authorities by noting that:

[s]ome government bodies have already emerged there spontaneously. Not only have they been recognised as the leadership of the

self-proclaimed republics – they have also become partners to the Minsk agreements and are taking part in the Contact Group alongside Kiev officials, enjoying the support of both Russia and the OSCE. Their representatives, Alexander Zakharchenko and Igor Plotnitsky, have signed a number of the Group's documents, and the Minsk agreements of 5 and 19 September. The elections to be held in the Donetsk and Lugansk People's Republics will be very important in terms of legitimising these authorities.[14]

Nonetheless, few, if any, of the provisions in the Minsk agreement of September 2014 came even close to implementation, and both sides increasingly worked towards consolidating and expanding their gains. This, in turn, intensified tensions and eventually led to renewed major escalation of fighting (see ahead). Consequently, a renewed international effort to achieve a political solution commenced in Minsk, resulting in the so-called Minsk II agreement of 12 February 2015.[15] Here, in addition to re-committing to a ceasefire, withdrawal of heavy weapons from the front line, etc., the sides agreed to carry out:

> constitutional reform in Ukraine with a new constitution entering into force by the end of 2015 providing for decentralization as a key element (including a reference to the specificities of certain areas in the Donetsk and Luhansk regions, agreed with the representatives of these areas), as well as adopting permanent legislation on the special status of certain areas of the Donetsk and Luhansk regions in line with measures as set out in the footnote until the end of 2015.[16]

The provisions in this footnote are significant in that they make concrete stipulations for future self-governance arrangements prior to any negotiations thereof, including the participation of local authorities in judicial appointments, the possibility of specific centre-periphery agreements on economic, social and cultural development, cross-border cooperation with regions in Russia, and locally controlled militia units – measures designed to strengthen and consolidate the status of Donbas as a 'special' region within Ukraine, thus legitimising its existence and its representatives. Put differently, from a Russian perspective, "the February 12 Minsk agreements, the Package of Measures for the Implementation of the Minsk Agreements and the declaration signed by our leaders in Minsk, set out exhaustively everything that needs to be done."[17]

While Minsk II remains unimplemented as well, its provisions clearly signal the extent to which Russia's position had shifted within a year – from a negotiated transition of uncertain outcome to a situation in which a fundamental territorial and political re-organisation of the Ukrainian state, quasi-constitutionally empowering and entrenching a strongly pro-Russian entity within Ukraine, was agreed in an ad-hoc international negotiation format. At the same time, the readiness of Ukraine's Western partners to accept these terms contrasts sharply with Ukraine's unwillingness to implement them. This, in turn, demonstrates an interesting dynamic of a blended conflict in a penetrated region: external actors exercise considerable influence over the dynamics of the conflict and its settlement process, but local actors are not without agency, either, and clearly have an ability to frustrate external 'designs.' This appears to be related, too, to the fact that, in the case of Ukraine, the regional context is characterised by antagonistic penetration; that is, the eastern Ukrainian conflict is partially overlaid with a broader conflict between Russia and the West. In terms of the conflict settlement process, this manifests itself in all involved actors having a shared interest in avoiding further hostile escalation but not enough of a shared interest in finding, and implementing, a sustainable settlement.

This state of affairs has affected the Ukrainian policy response at the domestic level, which, in turn, has further entrenched the deadlock in the conflict settlement process that has been one of the prevailing features of the crisis in Ukraine since Minsk II. Thus, the January 2018 Law of Ukraine "On particular features of state policy on providing the sovereignty of Ukraine on temporarily occupied territories of Donetsk and Luhansk oblasts"[18] delegates all responsibility for the protection of the civilian population in the rebel-controlled territories and their rights and freedoms, for the maintenance of public infrastructure, and for the provision of a wide range of social and public services to the Russian Federation. Legally entrenching the economic and social isolation of the rebel-controlled territories in domestic legislation and policy, the Law also draws its justification from international law, effectively supplementing Ukraine's claims against Russia in the International Court of Justice.[19] The law demonstrates Ukraine's determination to define the conflict in eastern Ukraine as Russian aggression and as an inter-state conflict, rather than, as previously proclaimed, an 'anti-terrorist operation.' While there is considerable justification in international law for such arguments, they do, however, undermine the Minsk agreements in which the DPR and LPR are defined as parties to the conflict (i.e., not Russia).

The change in the definition of the conflict is further cemented in Ukrainian domestic legislation with the almost simultaneously adopted Law 'On National Security of Ukraine,'[20] which changes the command structure of armed forces and security organisations in the zone of armed conflict (from 'Anti-Terrorist Operation' to 'Operation of Joint Forces') and assigns control to the Ministry of Defense rather than the Ministry of Interior. The national security law also establishes a threshold for military expenses in the state budget (minimum of 5% of GDP, including 3% to be spent on the Ukrainian armed forces), thus providing a long-term basis for the operation.

In addition, the draft of Law 8297 of 19 April 2018 "On the Changes to the Law of Ukraine 'On Citizenship of Ukraine'" submitted to the Verkhovna Rada by President Poroshenko stipulated conditions and procedures according to which residents of Crimea, Donetsk and Luhansk who cooperated with the 'occupational administrations' can be deprived of their Ukrainian citizenship. Although the draft law was subsequently withdrawn by Poroshenko on 16 May 2018, it nevertheless reflects a mindset that is strongly isolationist towards the rebel-controlled territories.[21] This policy may not be conducive to eventual reintegration of the country, but it is a popular view, especially in western and central Ukraine, where 64% and 51.5%, respectively, support the "termination of any relations (including economic ones) between Ukraine and uncontrolled territories of the Donbas."[22]

These and other legislative and policy initiatives indicate a significantly hardening position in Kyiv towards both Russia and the self-declared republics. They contribute to entrenching the current status quo of 'no peace, no war' in eastern Ukraine. Aimed at facilitating a strengthening of Ukraine's military potential, they do not, however, make this status quo more sustainable, and they are part of the dynamics which account for the fact that the implementation of the Minsk Agreements has become less and less likely. As such, they are a critical dimension of the background against which we can now assess the prospects of different conflict settlement scenarios.

Beyond failure? Three scenarios, their alternatives and the prospects for sustainable conflict settlement

Bearing in mind the particular local, regional and global dynamics of the conflict in and over Donbas, and the links between them, we begin our discussion of scenarios for conflict management and settlement with a number of general observations on how such territory-centred intra-state conflicts can be managed; that is, we briefly abstract from the notion that the conflict in Donbas is a more complex affair, captured in our notion of a blended conflict in an antagonistically penetrated region, and focus on just two of its core characteristics: namely, territorial contestation between government and separatists. In doing so, we focus primarily on recent European experiences,[23] including in the post-Soviet space, in order to offer context-relevant experiences.

With these caveats in mind, we can easily define a spectrum of possible conflict management and settlement options,[24] ranging from reintegration of Donbas into a unitary Ukrainian state (the status quo ante) to an (internationally mediated) negotiated secession of the rebel-controlled territories. An example of the former would be the reintegration of Serb-controlled territories in Croatia following a two-year transitional administration of these territories by a UN mission.[25] An example of the latter would be several other successor states of the former Yugoslavia: Bosnia and Herzegovina and Croatia, each of which experienced intense violent conflict on its path to internationally recognised statehood; Slovenia, where conflict was shorter and less bloody; and (the former Yugoslav republics of) Macedonia and Montenegro, whose secessions from Yugoslavia were not mired in violence. Between these two 'extremes' lie variations of three further scenarios:

1   Reintegration that accommodates separatist demands short of independence, by, for example, granting territorial autonomy or otherwise devolving competences from the centre to lower levels of authority (as, for example, in the Aland Islands, South Tyrol, and Gagauzia).
2   A stabilisation of territorial divisions with relatively low levels of violence, the maintenance or restoration of economic and humanitarian connectivity, and ongoing but inconclusive status negotiations, as, for example, in the so-called de-facto (or unrecognised) states in the post-Soviet region (Transnistria, and with some qualifications Nagorny Karabakh, as well as Abkhazia and South Ossetia before August 2008) and elsewhere (Northern Cyprus, Kosovo between 1999 and 2008).
3   An externally supported or imposed but contested change of international boundaries through annexation (Crimea) or (partial) recognition of unilaterally declared statehood (Kosovo, Abkhazia and South Ossetia since August 2008).

The current situation in Donbass most closely resembles the de-facto state scenario, despite the fact that the Minsk accords commit the conflict parties to some form of a reintegration scenario. The policy debate on the different options for managing and/or settling the conflict in Donbas generally reflects these different scenarios, but is primarily focused on three specific ones, which in turn represent particular interpretations of the broader scenarios outlined above. These three scenarios are the so-called Croatian scenario, Transnistrian scenario, and German scenario.[26]

The Croatian scenario

Ukrainian policy and expert communities describe the Croatian scenario as the reintegration of the DPR and LPR into a unitary, mono-lingual, and mono-ethnic Ukrainian state by military force. As the first-choice scenario for many of them, it implies a victory of Ukraine in a zero-sum game against

Russia-backed rebels. The Ukrainian government would restore its own rule in the rebel-controlled areas of Donetsk and Luhansk without making any concessions to the separatists, and rebels would be prosecuted according to Ukrainian legislation. In addition, Ukraine would claim compensation from Russia; even if no material compensation was forthcoming, this would still be a morale-boosting victory for the Ukrainian people; and, as a result, the Ukrainian nation-state and national identity would be strengthened and consolidated. This, in turn, implies a rejection of the Minsk accords on the grounds that it is unjust for the separatists, who are waging war against Ukraine, to have more rights and privileges than citizens in other provinces, and receive more international aid and investments, including secure funding from the state budget (Interviews 50, 53, 58–61, 63).

While this Croatian scenario remains the most popular among Ukrainian elites, civil society and the general public,[27] who, by and large, all reject compromise with Russia, its implementation is far from likely in the near future due to the military strength of the separatists and the continuing support they receive from Russia. Even if the military balance of power were to tilt in Ukraine's favour, any military campaign against the DPR and LPR would likely result in large-scale loss of human life and physical destruction, which would significantly impede any prospects for successful reintegration.

Consequently, the Croatian scenario, owing its inspiration to the United Nations Transitional Administration for Eastern Slavonia, Baranja and Western Sirmium, a two-year UN peacekeeping operation, is closely linked to debates on the deployment of UN peacekeepers to facilitate the reintegration of the current de-facto entities. While considerable enthusiasm had been expressed by several analysts and commentators in the West (International Crisis Group 2017, 2018; Melnyk and Umland 2016; Umland 2018; Vershbow 2018), as well as in Russia (Kortunbov 2017), that a UN mission could break the deadlock in the conflict in eastern Ukraine, the impasse between the local conflict parties and their respective external backers has not been resolved. A detailed proposal by the Hudson Institute in Washington (Gowan 2018) outlined how a twenty-thousand-strong UN-led military peacekeeping mission with significant EU and OSCE involvement in its police and civilian components might be able to facilitate the gradual reintegration of the currently rebel-controlled territories into Ukraine. Yet, the continuing divergence of opinion in Ukraine, Russia and the West over the strength and mandate of such a mission have seriously limited the prospects of this scenario.

Yet, it is not only this geopolitical obstacle which makes the Croatian scenario an unlikely one for the foreseeable future. A smaller number of our interviewees rejected the Croatian scenario also on the grounds that a more accommodating approach to reintegration should be adopted; that is, for a negotiated settlement along the lines of the Minsk accords with significant decentralisation of political power to Ukraine's regions (Interviews 27, 49, 62–64). While this is not incompatible with a UN-facilitated transition, it is critical to be mindful of the fact that such a more accommodating approach remains very much a minority view, including among Ukrainian citizens in the government-controlled areas of Donetsk and Luhansk, where only 14% support a special status for these regions within Ukraine or Russian a second state language.[28] As long as Ukrainian politics and public opinion continue to adopt a hard-line approach that is unwilling to accept compromises and concessions, the incentives for separatists, and more so for Russia, to embrace reintegration under these conditions are almost non-existent. Special status matters for them both: for the separatists, a minimum of meaningful territorial self-governance is essential, while for Russia, it is important that the two de-facto entities can significant political exercise influence in Kyiv after any reintegration such that they continue to be useful proxies for Russian policy in the contested neighbourhood (see Malyarenko and Wolff 2018).

The Transnistrian scenario

This scenario is shorthand for a compromise between Ukraine and the de-facto entities (and thus, implicitly, Russia) that would confer a degree of legitimacy onto the DPR and LPR and allow for their partial economic reintegration with Ukraine. As the experience of Moldova and Transnistria demonstrates, such a 'frozen conflict' situation has both advantages and disadvantages for the principal stakeholders, although the former, by and large, outweigh the latter. Our interviewees (Interviews 51–54, 58–63) suggested that the list of gains for Ukraine includes a more stable ceasefire, the possibility to receive international aid for the rehabilitation of Donbas, and benefits from increased and more regulated trade with the people's republics and Russia, as well as an improvement in relations with Russia more generally. However, there is also an acknowledgement that ruling elites in Kyiv would suffer reputational losses among the so-called patriotic segments of Ukrainian society (possibly strengthening radical-right political parties). Given the de-facto nature of this scenario, the situation would remain vulnerable to both changes in the geopolitical situation and in domestic politics in Russia and Ukraine. While the situation in Moldova/Transnistria has remained overall stable since the signing of the 1992 ceasefire agreement, events in Abkhazia and South Ossetia highlight the potential volatility of such an arrangement (Interviews 28–30, 37, 39, 53, 54).

The German scenario

As understood by Kyiv, this scenario implies the legal acknowledgement of the status of the DPR and LPR as occupied territories and consequently a full ban on all relations with them, including the denial of Ukrainian citizenship to residents of the people's republics and a full economic and transport blockade of the rebel-controlled territories.[29] This scenario, in loose analogy to German reunification, does not rule out the reintegration of the de-facto entities into the Ukrainian state but rather makes it contingent upon the currently prevailing geopolitical conditions changing. However, it is unclear whether the complete isolation of the rebel-controlled areas of Donetsk and Luhansk is possible – or even desirable. There is no guarantee that the policy of isolation to be pursued much more vigorously and comprehensively by Kyiv if the German scenario were implemented would bring about a sustainable end to the violence that continuous to pierce the ceasefire. Nor is it clear what the impact would be of such a policy on the Ukrainian economy which still depends on Russian markets and some form of economic exchanges with the occupied territories (Interviews 28–30, 37, 39, 40, 55–58, 60–63).

Alternative scenarios

While not widely discussed in public, recent experience indicates that at least one other scenario is plausible: namely, the externally supported or imposed but contested change of international boundaries. This is particularly relevant given Russia's annexation of Crimea and its recognition of the unilaterally declared statehood of Abkhazia and South Ossetia following the Russian-Georgian war of August 2008.

A Crimean or Georgian scenario would require a clear decision in Moscow and, given the Kremlin's Crimean experience, also require a preparedness to absorb the costs and consequences of such actions. Thus, both our Russian and Ukrainian interlocutors see a relatively high threshold that would need to be crossed before this scenario might be activated. Russian experts suggest that such conditions could include a military operation of the Ukrainian army in Donbas (such as under the Croatian scenario), the building of an American or NATO military base in Ukraine, or a clear path for Ukraine's accession to NATO (Interviews 28, 29, 37, Workshops G, H).[30] Whereas the Crimean scenario looks the more unlikely of these two scenarios (due to the high probability of more painful anti-Russian economic sanctions), a 'Georgian scenario' may be considered more feasible, especially if Ukraine were to move down the path of the German scenario (Interview 28).

That said, whereas recognising the independence of Abkhazia and Ossetia favoured the relative stabilisation of relations between Georgia and the two unrecognised republics (and subsequently, Russia), a possible recognition of LPR and DPR cannot guarantee stable peace in Donbas as Russia would have to compensate for its loss of influence on Ukraine (compared to, for example, the Transnistrian scenario) with other means of destabilisation, such as the continuation of low-intensity but persistent breaches of the ceasefire and other forms of direct and indirect interference in Ukraine (such as economic disruption, use of cyber warfare, etc.). In this context, it is important to bear in mind that Ukraine remains a very weak state and highly vulnerable to such other forms of destabilisation. With at best weak economic growth, high unemployment despite a massive brain drain, increasing poverty and deepening socio-economic inequality, Ukraine has been unable to establish effective institutions governed by the rule of law. In addition, violent organised crime networks have flourished, partly due to the uncontrolled smuggling of arms from the conflict zone. The resulting loss of legitimacy and public trust in the post-Maidan government in Kyiv has, thus, created new opportunities for Russia to shape domestic politics in Ukraine beyond Donbas.

Considering further that the general and very acrimonious volatility of relations between Russia and the West, and increasing divisions in the West itself, are unlikely to facilitate a pro-Russian settlement in the near future, while simultaneously, a strongly anti-Russian government and similar public sentiment has emerged in Ukraine, a shift in Russia's perceptions of how best to secure its long-term interests cannot be completely cast aside. An indication that a positive perception of the Georgian and Crimean scenarios might be gaining ground is a lengthy interview given by the president of the Russian National Strategy Institute, Mikhail Remizov, to the Russian Federal News agency in which he argues for the step-by-step recognition of the DPR and LPR.[31] Remizov points out that the population of Donbas is psychologically unprepared to live for long in unrecognised states, which is likely to result in dissatisfaction and consequent mass protests. Additionally, dissatisfaction is likely to increase emigration, especially among the highly skilled segment of the local labour force, further inhibiting prospects of economic recovery and sustainable growth that are already hampered by war-related destruction of infrastructure, the disruption of economic activity and high levels of corruption among the republican authorities. Thus, rather than subsidising the rebel-controlled territories, Russian interests would be much better served by investments in their economic development, which, in turn, would be predicated on their full or partial recognition.

While such views might be gaining some traction, for the time being, Russian control of Donbas remains Moscow's main tool of leverage over Ukraine. That the Georgian and Crimean scenarios are, therefore, relatively undesirable from a Russian perspective is also confirmed by our Ukrainian interlocutors (Interviews 19, 27). From a Ukrainian perspective, the isolation of rebel-controlled Donbas (as envisaged under the German scenario) is a factor of stabilisation as it facilitates political and socio-economic rehabilitation and regime consolidation in the rest of Ukraine by severely limiting the leverage that Russia can exercise through the rebel-controlled territories.

Notes

1 Simultaneously, Russia prepared and executed the annexation of Crimea. We do not cover this particular sequence of events in our analysis, as Russia here pursued a very distinct approach, solely focused on the annexation of the peninsula and driven by military-strategic and political considerations that were distinct from those underpinning the Russian approach in mainland eastern Ukraine and addressed a particularly critical Russian security concern, namely securing its naval base in Sevastopol.

2 See also Malyarenko (2015).

3 Similar to the situation in Georgia in 2008, it is, however, also conceivable that Russia may eventually decide to consolidate its gains and either recognise the two entities or, like Crimea, annex them.

4 "Agreement on the settlement of crisis in Ukraine", www.auswaertiges-amt. de/blob/260130/db4f5326f21530cad8d351152feb5e26/140221-ukr-erklaerung-data.pdf (accessed 24 September 2018).

5 As Yanukovych realised that the Euromaidan movement did not accept the agreement, he went to Kharkov to a meeting of all deputies of local councils. Unable to obtain their support, he escaped to Russia.

6 "Statement by the Russian Ministry of Foreign Affairs regarding the events in Ukraine", 24 February 2014, www.mid.ru/en/foreign_policy/news/-/asset_publisher/cKNonkJE02Bw/content/id/73918 (accessed 24 September 2018).

7 "Geneva Statement on Ukraine", https://geneva.usmission.gov/2014/04/18/text-of-the-geneva-statement-on-ukraine-released-by-the-us-eu-ukraine-and-russia/ (accessed 24 September 2018).

8 "Statement by the Russian Ministry of Foreign Affairs regarding the aggravation of the situation in the South-Eastern regions of Ukraine", 13 April 2014, www.mid.ru/en/press_service/spokesman/official_statement/-/asset_publisher/t2GCdmD8RNIr/content/id/65894 (accessed 24 September 2018).

9 For example, "Interview of the Russian Foreign Minister Sergey Lavrov with ITAR-TASS", 10 September 2014, www.mid.ru/en/press_service/minister_speeches/-/asset_publisher/7OvQR5KJWVmR/content/id/671172 (accessed 24 September 2018) and "Foreign Minister Sergey Lavrov delivers a speech and answers questions during debates at the 51st Munich Security Conference", Munich, February 7, 2015, www.mid.ru/en/press_service/minister_speeches/-/asset_publisher/7OvQR5KJWVmR/content/id/949358 (accessed 24 September 2018).

10 See "Speech by the Russian Foreign Minister Sergey Lavrov and his answers to questions from the mass media summarising the meeting with EU, Russian, US and Ukrainian representatives", Geneva, 17 April 2014, www.mid.ru/en/press_service/minister_speeches/-/asset_publisher/7OvQR5KJWVmR/content/id/64910 (accessed 24 September 2018).

11 For a more detailed exploration of OSCE activities during this period, see Zannier (2015).

12 See "Protocol on the results of consultations of the Trilateral Contact Group with respect to the joint steps aimed at the implementation of the Peace Plan of the President of Ukraine, P. Poroshenko, and the initiatives of the President of Russia, V. Putin", available at http://stefanwolff.com/wp-content/uploads/2018/01/Full-text-of-the-Minsk-I-agreement-English.pdf (accessed 2 November 2018).

13 Interview given by the Russian Foreign Minister, Sergey Lavrov, to the "Russia Today" TV channel and "Vesti nedeli" on "Rossiya" TV Channel, New York, 27 September 2013; www.mid.ru/en/press_service/minister_speeches/-/asset_publisher/7OvQR5KJWVmR/content/id/668812 (accessed 24 September 2018).

14 "Foreign Minister Sergey Lavrov's interview with Life News television and Izvestia daily", Moscow, 27 October 2014 www.mid.ru/en/press_service/minister_speeches/-/asset_publisher/7OvQR5KJWVmR/content/id/742828 (accessed 24 September 2018).

15 "Package of measures for the implementation of the Minsk agreements", https://peacemaker.un.org/ukraine-minsk-implementation15 (accessed 24 September 2018).

16 "Package of measures for the implementation of the Minsk agreements", https://peacemaker.un.org/ukraine-minsk-implementation15 (accessed 24 September 2018).

17 "Foreign Minister Sergey Lavrov's comment for the media on the results of a Normandy format meeting", Paris, 24 February 2015, www.mid.ru/en/press_service/minister_speeches/-/asset_publisher/7OvQR5KJWVmR/content/id/961334 (accessed 24 September 2018).

18 See "Про особливості державної політики із забезпечення державного суверенітету України на тимчасово окупованих територіях у Донецькій та Луганській областях", Документ 2268-VIII, чинний, поточна редакція–Прийняття від, 18 January 2018, http://zakon.rada.gov.ua/laws/show/2268-19 (accessed 24 September 2018).

19 See "Application instituting proceedings filed in the registry of the court on 16 January 2017", International Court of Justice, www.icj-cij.org/files/case-related/166/19314.pdf (accessed 24 September 2018).

20 See "Про національну безпеку України", Документ 2469-VIII, чинний, поточна редакція – Прийняття від, 21 June 2018, http://zakon.rada.gov.ua/laws/show/2469-viii (accessed 24 September 2018).

21 See "Проект Закону про внесення змін до Закону України 'Про громадянство України' щодо удосконалення окремих положень", w1.c1.rada.gov.ua/pls/zweb2/webproc4_1?pf3511=63900 (accessed 24 September 2018). See also "Poroshenko withdraws bill on stripping of Ukrainian citizenship for voting in Russian-occupied Crimea", *UNIAN Information Agency*, 16 May 2018, www.unian.info/politics/10119431-poroshenko-withdraws-bill-on-stripping-of-ukrainian-citizenship-for-voting-in-russian-occupied-crimea.html (accessed 24 September 2018) and "Poroshenko withdraws citizenship bill from parliament", *Interfax-Ukraine*, 16 May 2018, https://en.interfax.com.ua/news/general/505663.html (accessed 24 September 2018).

22 See poll of 2021 respondents conducted by the Razumkov Center in February 2016 in all regions of Ukraine, except Crimea and the rebel-controlled areas

of Donbas. http://old.razumkov.org.ua/ukr/poll.php?poll_id=1110 (accessed 24 September 2018). The policy of isolation was less popular in southern and eastern Ukraine, where 24.2% and 32.9% of respondents supported it. The level of support in government-controlled areas of Donbas was 33.9%.

23 See also Csergö, Roseberry, and Wolff (2017) and Wolff (2013).

24 For a comprehensive discussion of conflict management and settlement, see Wolff and Yakinthou (2013); for different typologies, see Coakley (1992) and McGarry, O'Leary, and Simeon (2008).

25 The United Nations Transitional Administration for Eastern Slavonia, Baranja and Western Sirmium (UNTAES), and the challenges of this approach are analysed in Boothby (2004).

26 See for example, Gushchin et al. (2016) and Markedonov (2014, 2015). See also Vladimir Gorbulin, "Гибридная война: все только начинается . . .", 25 March 2016, https://zn.ua/internal/gibridnaya-voyna-vse-tolko-nachinaetsya-_.html (accessed 24 September 2018); Vladimir Gorbulin, "Есть ли жизнь после Минска?", 12 February 2016, https://zn.ua/internal/est-li-zhizn-posle-minska-razmyshleniya-o-neizbezhnosti-neobhodimyh-izmeneniy-_.html (accessed 24 September 2018); Vladimir Gorbulin, "Пять сценариев для украино-российских отношений", 19 June 2015, https://zn.ua/internal/pyat-scenariev-dlya-ukraino-rossiyskih-otnosheniy-_.html (accessed 24 September 2018).

27 "Лідерство України у Мінському процесі–результати соціологічного опитування 'Кальміуської групи'", *GfK Ukraine*, 10 July 2018, www.gfk.com/uk-ua/rishennja/news/kalmius-group-survey/ (accessed 24 September 2018).

28 See July 2017 survey results reported at http://dif.org.ua/article/gromadska-dumka-naselennya-donbasu-lipen2017 (accessed 24 September 2018).

29 This is, of course, a very limited interpretation of the German scenario covering the period of the so-called Hallstein doctrine in the 1950s and first half of the 1960s, rather than the gradual rapprochement between West and East Germany under *Ostpolitik*, which ultimately proved a more successful approach to reunification. See Wolff (2003).

30 See also summaries of interviews with Russia-based experts: "Донбасс надолго останется 'серой зоной'", 17 March 2017, www.rosbalt.ru/world/2017/03/17/1599769.html (accessed 24 September 2018) and "Эксперты представили три сценария развития ситуации в Донбассе", 2 July 2015, www.rosbalt.ru/ukraina/2015/07/02/1414847.html (accessed 24 September 2018).

31 "Михаил Ремизов: Пора делать шаги в сторону признания ДНР и ЛНР", Interview with Mikhail Remizov, 17 January 2017, https://riafan.ru/595883-mihail-remizov-pora-delat-shagi-v-storonu-priznaniya-dnr-i-lnr (accessed 24 September 2018).

7   Conclusion

Ukraine has been faced with fundamental challenges to its sovereignty and territorial integrity since the end of 2013. Over the five years since the beginning of the Euromaidan revolution, the country has seen part of its territory annexed by Russia (the Crimean peninsula) and has fought a civil war against Russian-backed rebels in the Donbas region. This latter challenge was the focus of our analysis in this book which sought to trace the emergence of two new de-facto entities on the territory of Ukraine, the so-called people's republics of Donetsk and Luhansk.

Characterising this particular conflict as a blended conflict in an antagonistically penetrated region, we investigated how local, state, regional and global dynamics interacted and led to a situation in which Ukraine remains a deeply divided and fragile state. While we recognise the very contemporary causes of the conflict and its outcomes so far, we also acknowledge that current developments, to some extent, have their roots in the recent and not so recent past – in this case, the incomplete state- and nation-building processes in Ukraine since the country's independence in 1991 and its complicated relationships with Russia and the West, which are in turn embedded in the increasing tensions between these two increasingly antagonistic actors whose geopolitical and geo-economic rivalries, in part, play out in and over Ukraine.

Against this background, Ukraine is now confronted with two relatively consolidated, Russian-protected de-facto entities on its territory and few prospects for their meaningful reintegration in the foreseeable future. As attitudes among political elites and ordinary Ukrainians have grown more hostile towards Russia and more isolationist towards the Donetsk and Luhansk people's republics, a volatile status quo has emerged on the ground which demonstrates that the various sides in this conflict have reached a dead end with their policies. The separatists in Donbas have not achieved statehood or annexation by Russia, while Ukraine has been unable (and seems increasingly unwilling) to reach a settlement that would facilitate reintegration.

Ukrainian citizens appear equally unwilling to fight and to compromise, thus effectively settling for a situation in which the government can rely on their support for a policy that isolates the self-declared republics economically while offering some humanitarian support to IDPs from, and the remaining population in, rebel-controlled Donbas.[1] At the same time, Russian influence on the geopolitical orientation of Ukraine towards the West, which was arguably at the core of the initial Maidan conflict, has significantly decreased. Meanwhile, Western aspirations for reforms and democratic consolidation in Ukraine have also not been fulfilled.

As a consequence, a stalemate has been reached at every level of our analysis – from the local situation in Donbas, to the state-wide dynamics in Ukraine as a whole, and to the regional and global dynamics of geopolitical and geo-economic competition between Russia and the West. Still pierced by occasionally escalating, albeit generally low, levels of violence in Donbas, this situation does not bode well for stability in the post-Soviet region and the contested neighbourhood between Russia and the West. Moreover, new confrontations loom in the already volatile Black Sea region, with NATO members Romania and Bulgaria (who are simultaneously also part of the EU), and Turkey, on its western and southern shores, Ukraine and Russia in the north, and Georgia, including the separatist region of Abkhazia, in the east. While NATO has responded to Russia's annexation of Crimea and support for the self-declared republics in Donbas in the past (Anastasov 2018), the completion of Russia's land link with Crimea in the form of a 12-mile bridge across the Kerch Strait poses a new set of challenges, with Russia effectively occupying the Sea of Azov and illegally limiting access to the Ukrainian port of Mariupol and prompting Ukraine to threaten to annul a 2008 cooperation treaty with Russia on use of the Sea of Azov and Kerch Strait.[2] This increases both Ukraine's economic vulnerability and the potential for conflict escalation, especially along the northern shores of the Sea of Azov where Ukraine still holds strategically important territory separating the rebel-controlled areas of Donbas from Crimea. This evolving threat has prompted, for example, the UK to extend its training programme for the Ukrainian armed forces for another two years and to commit to the additional deployment of Royal Marines in 2018 and Royal Navy patrols in 2019.[3]

For the time being, thus, it appears that all sides in this conflict seem to be willing to accept this new status quo without formally recognising it. As distrust remains the predominant characteristic of the relationships among all the different actors across the various interlocking confrontations in this blended conflict, the different sides also remain locked into a security dilemma in which they are all increasing their readiness to defend the current state of affairs while preparing for future opportunities to enhance their own position vis-à-vis their adversaries. Apart from the tremendous human costs that this imposes on Ukraine's citizens, this situation bears the seeds of undermining its own long-term sustainability – not merely in the context of the crisis in Ukraine, but potentially across the post-Soviet space from the Baltic Sea to the Caspian Sea.

Notes

1 See "Наступать не хотим, поступаться не будем: как украинцы видят прекращение войны на Донбассе", *Realist Online*, 7 September 2018, https://realist.online/article/nastupat-ne-hotim-postupatsya-ne-budem-kak-ukraincy-vidyat-prekrashenie-vojny-na-donbasse (accessed 24 September 2018).

2 "Немедленно денонсировать Договор между Украиной и РФ о сотрудничестве в использовании Азовского моря и Керченского пролива", *Зеркало Недели*, 9 June 2018, https://zn.ua/internal/okkupaciya-azova-286235_.html (accessed 24 September 2018).

3 See "Defence Secretary announces extension of support to Ukraine's Armed Forces", *UK Ministry of Defence*, 21 September 2018, www.gov.uk/government/news/defence-secretary-announces-extension-of-support-to-ukraines-armed-forces (accessed 24 September 2018); and "Gavin Williamson commits extra British troops in Ukraine to stop Russia 'reversing Cold War outcome'", *The Telegraph*, 20 September 2018, www.telegraph.co.uk/news/2018/09/20/gavin-williamson-commits-extra-british-troops-ukraine-stop-russia/ (accessed 24 September 2018). On Ukrainian reception of the UK commitment, see "Великобритания расширит военное присутствие в Черном море", *Зеркало Недели*, 22 September 2018, https://zn.ua/UKRAINE/velikobritaniya-rasshirit-voennoe-prisutstvie-v-chernom-more-295282_.html (accessed 24 September 2018).

References

Allison, Roy. 2014. 'Russian "Deniable" Intervention in Ukraine: How and Why Russia Broke the Rules'. *International Affairs* 90(6): 1255–97. http://dx.doi.org/10.1111/1468-2346.12170.

Anastasov, Pavel. 2018. 'The Black Sea Region: A Critical Intersection'. *NATO Review*. www.nato.int/docu/review/2018/Also-in-2018/the-black-sea-region-a-critical-intersection-nato-security/EN/index.htm.

Auer, Stefan. 2015. 'Carl Schmitt in the Kremlin: The Ukraine Crisis and the Return of Geopolitics'. *International Affairs* 91(5): 953–68. http://dx.doi.org/10.1111/1468-2346.12392.

Ayoob, Mohammed. 1999. 'From Regional System to Regional Society: Exploring Key Variables in the Construction of Regional Order'. *Australian Journal of International Affairs* 53(3): 247–60. www.tandfonline.com/doi/full/10.1080/00049919993845 (September 16, 2018).

Bakke, Kristin M., and Erik Wibbels. 2006. 'Diversity, Disparity, and Civil Conflict in Federal States'. *World Politics* 59(1): 1–50.

Bercovitch, Jacob. 2003. 'Managing Internationalized Ethnic Conflict: Evaluating the Role and Relevance of Mediation'. *World Affairs* 166(1): 56–68. www.jstor.org/stable/20672677 (September 16, 2018).

Beyer, John, and Stefan Wolff. 2016. 'Linkage, Leverage, and Moldova's Transnistria Problem'. *East European Politics* 32(335–354).

Boothby, Derek. 2004. 'Political Challenges of Administering Eastern Slavonia'. *Global Governance* 10: 37–52.

Brown, Michael E. 2001. 'The Causes and Regional Dimensions of Internal Conflict'. In *The International Dimensions of Internal Conflict*, ed. Michael E. Brown. Cambridge, MA: The MIT Press, 571–601.

Buhaug, Halvard. 2006. 'Relative Capability and Rebel Objective in Civil War'. *Journal of Peace Research* 43(6): 691–708. http://journals.sagepub.com/doi/10.1177/0022343306069255 (April 9, 2018).

Buhaug, Halvard, Scott Gates, and Päivi Lujala. 2009. 'Geography, Rebel Capability, and the Duration of Civil Conflict'. *Journal of Conflict Resolution* 53(4): 544–69. http://jcr.sagepub.com/cgi/content/abstract/53/4/544.

Buhaug, Halvard, and Jan Ketil Rød. 2006. 'Local Determinants of African Civil Wars, 1970–2001'. *Political Geography* 25(3): 315–35. www.sciencedirect.com/science/article/pii/S0962629806000205.

Bunce, Valerie, and Aida Hozic. 2015. 'Hybrid Regimes and International Aggression'. *Comparative Democratization* 13(1): 15–18. www.compdem.org/wp-content/uploads/2015/07/February-2015-APSA-CD.pdf.

Buzan, Barry, and Ole Waever. 2003. *Regions and Powers: The Structure of International Security*. Cambridge: Cambridge University Press.

Cadier, David. 2014. 'Eastern Partnership vs Eurasian Union? The EU–Russia Competition in the Shared Neighbourhood and the Ukraine Crisis'. *Global Policy* 5: 76–85. http://dx.doi.org/10.1111/1758-5899.12152.

Cederman, Lars-Erik, Halvard Buhaug, and Jan Ketil Rød. 2009. 'Ethno-Nationalist Dyads and Civil War: A GIS-Based Analysis'. *Journal of Conflict Resolution* 53(4): 496–525. http://jcr.sagepub.com/content/53/4/496.abstract.

Cederman, Lars-Erik, Luc Girardin, and Kristian Skrede Gleditsch. 2009. 'Ethno-Nationalist Triads: Assessing the Influence of Kin Groups on Civil Wars'. *World Politics* 61(3): 403–37.

Cederman, Lars-Erik, Andreas Wimmer, and Brian Min. 2010. 'Why Do Ethnic Groups Rebel? New Data and Analysis'. *World Politics* 62(1): 87–119. http://dx.doi.org/10.1017/S0043887109990219.

Charap, Samuel. 2014a. 'The Ukraine Impasse'. *Survival* 56(5): 225–32. http://dx.doi.org/10.1080/00396338.2014.962813.

———. 2014b. 'Ukraine: Seeking an Elusive New Normal'. *Survival* 56(3): 85–94. http://dx.doi.org/10.1080/00396338.2014.920140.

Charap, Samuel, and Keith Darden. 2014. 'Russia and Ukraine'. *Survival* 56(2): 7–14. http://dx.doi.org/10.1080/00396338.2014.901726.

Cleary, Laura. 2016. 'Half Measures and Incomplete Reforms: The Breeding Ground for a Hybrid Civil Society in Ukraine'. *Southeast European and Black Sea Studies* 16(1): 7–23. https://doi.org/10.1080/14683857.2016.1148410.

Coakley, John 1992. 'The Resolution of Ethnic Conflict: Towards a Typology'. *International Political Science Review* 13(4): 343–58.

Collier, Paul, and Anke Hoeffler. 1998. 'On Economic Causes of Civil War'. *Oxford Economic Papers* 50(4): 563–73.

———. 2004. 'Greed and Grievance in Civil War'. *Oxford Economic Papers* 56: 563–95.

———. 2005. 'Resource Rents, Governance, and Conflict'. *Journal of Conflict Resolution* 49(4): 625–33. http://jcr.sagepub.com/cgi/content/abstract/49/4/625.

Coppedge, Michael. 2012. *Strategies for Social Inquiry: Democratization and Research Methods*. Cambridge: Cambridge University Press. www.cambridge.org/core/books/democratization-and-research-methods/2F9270122CA9AB8D698ADC94942DB146.

Cordell, Karl, and Stefan Wolff. 2009. *Ethnic Conflict: Causes–Consequences–Responses*. Polity: Cambridge.

Csergő, Zsuzsa, Philippe Roseberry, and Stefan Wolff. 2017. 'Institutional Outcomes of Territorial Contestation: Lessons from Post-Communist Europe, 1989–2012'. *Publius: The Journal of Federalism* 47.

Cybriwsky, Roman. 2014. 'Kyiv's Maidan: From Duma Square to Sacred Space'. *Eurasian Geography and Economics* 55(3): 270–85. https://doi.org/10.1080/15387216.2014.991341

Deiwiks, Christa, Lars-Erik Cederman, and Kristian Skrede Gleditsch. 2012. 'Inequality and Conflict in Federations'. *Journal of Peace Research* 49(2): 289–304. http://jpr.sagepub.com/cgi/content/abstract/49/2/289.

Deliagin, Mikhail, Pyotr Alexandrov-Derkachenko, Yuri Boldyrev, Konstantin Zatulin, Fyodor Lukyanov, and Semyon Uralov. 2015. 'What Is Happening in Ukraine and What Kind of Future Awaits It?'. *Russian Politics & Law* 53(1): 5–46. http://dx.doi.org/10.1080/10611940.2015.1042342.

Diprose, Rachael. 2009. 'Decentralization, Horizontal Inequalities and Conflict Management in Indonesia'. *Ethnopolitics* 8(1): 107–34. http://dx.doi.org/10.1080/17449050902738804.

Diprose, Rachael, and Ukoha Ukiwo. 2008. *Decentralisation and Conflict Management in Indonesia and Nigeria*. Oxford: Centre for Research on Inequality, Human Security and Ethnicity. http://r4d.dfid.gov.uk/PDF/Outputs/Inequality/wp49.pdf.

Dunn, Elizabeth Cullen, and Michael S. Bobick. 2014. 'The Empire Strikes Back: War without War and Occupation without Occupation in the Russian Sphere of Influence'. *American Ethnologist* 41(3): 405–13. http://dx.doi.org/10.1111/amet.12086.

Dutch Safety Board. 2015. 'Investigation Crash MH17, 17 July 2014'. 22 April 2016. http://onderzoeksraad.nl/en/onderzoek/2049/investigation-crash-mh17-17-july-2014.

Ehteshami, Anoushiravan, and Süleyman Elik. 2011. 'Turkey's Growing Relations with Iran and Arab Middle East'. *Turkish Studies* 12(4): 643–62. http://dx.doi.org/10.1080/14683849.2011.624322.

Fearon, James D. 2005. 'Primary Commodity Exports and Civil War'. *Journal of Conflict Resolution* 49(4): 483–507. http://jcr.sagepub.com/cgi/content/abstract/49/4/483.

Fearon, James D., and David D. Laitin. 2003. 'Ethnicity, Insurgency, and Civil War'. *American Political Science Review* 97(1): 75–90.

———. 2008. 'Civil War Termination'. *Annual Meeting of the American Political Science Association*. https://web.stanford.edu/group/fearon-research/cgi-bin/wordpress/wp-content/uploads/2013/10/civil-war-termination.pdf.

Fedorenko, Kostyantyn, Olena Rybiy, and Andreas Umland. 2016. 'The Ukrainian Party System before and after the 2013–2014 Euromaidan'. *Europe-Asia Studies* 68(4): 609–30. https://doi.org/10.1080/09668136.2016.1174981.

Feklyunina, Valentina. 2015. 'Soft Power and Identity: Russia, Ukraine and the "Russian World(S)"'. *European Journal of International Relations*. http://ejt.sagepub.com/cgi/content/abstract/1354066115601200v1.

Fitzpatrick, Mark. 2014. 'The Ukraine Crisis and Nuclear Order'. *Survival* 56(4): 81–90. http://dx.doi.org/10.1080/00396338.2014.941552.

Freedman, Lawrence. 2014. 'Ukraine and the Art of Limited War'. *Survival* 56(6): 7–38. http://dx.doi.org/10.1080/00396338.2014.985432.

Gagnon, Valère Philip. 2004. *The Myth of Ethnic War: Serbia and Croatia in the 1990s*. Ithaka, NY: Cornell University Press. https://books.google.co.uk/books?hl=en&lr=&id=6vbz_WMRiwEC&oi=fnd&pg=PR7&dq=gagnon+ethnic+conflict&ots=Go5eLpmoXZ&sig=cAP_M0eRw4H_cCrMPpT3SWXZvAI#v=onepage&q=gagnonethnicconflict&f=false (September 16, 2018).

Gardner, Hall. 2016. 'The Russian Annexation of Crimea: Regional and Global Ramifications'. *European Politics and Society* 17(4): 490–505. http://dx.doi.org/10.1080/23745118.2016.1154190.

George, Alexander L., and Andrew Bennett. 2005. *Case Studies and Theory Development in the Social Sciences*. Cambridge, MA: MIT Press. https://mitpress.mit.edu/books/case-studies-and-theory-development-social-sciences (August 16, 2018).

German, Tracey. 2016. 'Russia and South Ossetia: Conferring Statehood or Creeping Annexation?'. *Southeast European and Black Sea Studies* 16(1): 155–67. http://dx.doi.org/10.1080/14683857.2016.1148411.

Gerring, John. 2007. *Case Study Research: Principles and Practices*. New York, NY: Cambridge University Press.

———. 2012. *Social Science Methodology: A Unified Framework*. Cambridge: Cambridge University Press. https://books.google.co.uk/books?hl=en&lr=&id=kE7TyioDHiUC&oi=fnd&pg=PR7&dq=gerring+2012+social+science&ots=2Nutl2Bewv&sig=VR586MpgmWCfJA8zPIDc9tb7QA8#v=onepage&q=gerring 2012socialscience&f=false (September 16, 2018).

Gerrits, Andre W. M., and Max Bader. 2016. 'Russian Patronage over Abkhazia and South Ossetia: Implications for Conflict Resolution'. *East European Politics* 32(3): 297–313. http://dx.doi.org/10.1080/21599165.2016.1166104.

Glaurdić, Josip. 2016. 'Yugoslavia's Dissolution: Between the Scylla of Facts and the Charybdis of Interpretation'. In *Debating the End of Yugoslavia*, ed. Florian Bieber and Armina Galijaš. London: Routledge, 23–38. www.taylorfrancis.com/books/e/9781317154242/chapters/10.4324%2F9781315576039-3 (September 16, 2018).

Götz, Elias. 2015. 'It's Geopolitics, Stupid: Explaining Russia's Ukraine Policy'. *Global Affairs* 1(1): 3–10. http://dx.doi.org/10.1080/23340460.2015.960184.

Gowan, Richard. 2018. *Can the United Nations Unite Ukraine?* Washington, D.C.: Hudson Insititute.

Gurr, Ted Robert. 1993. 'Why Minorities Rebel: A Global Analysis of Communal Mobilization and Conflict since 1945'. *International Political Science Review* 14(2): 161–201.

Gurr, Ted Robert, and Will H. Moore. 1997. 'Ethnopolitical Rebellion: A Cross-Sectional Analysis of the 1980s with Risk Assessments for the 1990s'. *American Journal of Political Science* 41(4): 1079–103. www.jstor.org/stable/2960482.

Gushchin, Alexander W., Artem G. Dankov, Sergey M. Markedonov, and Sergey W. Rekeda. 2016. *Конфликты На Постсоветском Пространстве: Перспективы Урегулирования и Роль России (Conflicts in the Post-Soviet Space: Prospects for a Settlement and the Role of Russia)*. Moscow: Russian Council on International Affairs. http://russiancouncil.ru/common/upload/Postsoviet-Conflicts-Paper36-ru.pdf.

Haukkala, Hiski. 2015. 'From Cooperative to Contested Europe? The Conflict in Ukraine as a Culmination of a Long-Term Crisis in EU–Russia Relations'. *Journal of Contemporary European Studies* 23(1): 25–40. http://dx.doi.org/10.1080/14782804.2014.1001822.

Hopf, Ted. 2016. '"Crimea Is Ours": A Discursive History'. *International Relations* 30(2): 227–55. http://ire.sagepub.com/content/30/2/227.abstract.

Horlubin, Volodymyr Pavlovych, Vlasiuk, E. Libanova, and O. Liashenko. 2016. *Donbas and Crimea: Return at What Price?* Kyiv: NISS.

Horowitz, Donald L. 1985. *Ethnic Groups in Conflict*. Berkeley, CA: University of California Press.

Hughes, James, and Gwendolyn Sasse. 2016. 'Power Ideas and Conflict: Ideology, Linkage and Leverage in Crimea and Chechnya'. *East European Politics* 32(3): 314–34. http://dx.doi.org/10.1080/21599165.2015.1124091.

Humphreys, Macartan. 2005. 'Natural Resources, Conflict, and Conflict Resolution: Uncovering the Mechanisms'. *Journal of Conflict Resolution* 49(4): 508–37. http://jcr.sagepub.com/cgi/content/abstract/49/4/508.

International Crisis Group. 2017. *Can Peacekeepers Break the Deadlock in Ukraine?* Brussels. https://d2071andvip0wj.cloudfront.net/246-can-peacekeepers-break-the-deadlock-in-ukraine.pdf (September 15, 2018).

———. 2018. *Peacekeeping in Ukraine's Donbas: Opportunities and Risks | Crisis Group*. Brussels. www.crisisgroup.org/europe-central-asia/eastern-europe/ukraine/donbas-peacekeeping-opportunities-and-risks (September 15, 2018).

International Federation for Human Rights and Center for Civil Liberties. 2015. *Eastern Ukraine: Civilians Caught in the Crossfire*. Paris: International Federation for Human Rights. www.fidh.org/IMG/pdf/eastern_ukraine-ld.pdf.

International Partnership for Human Rights. 2015. *Fighting Impunity in Eastern Ukraine*. Brussels: International Partnership for Human Rights. http://iphronline.org/wp-content/uploads/2015/10/Fighting-impunity-in-Eastern-Ukraine-October-2015.pdf.

Ishchenko, Volodymyr. 2016. 'Far Right Participation in the Ukrainian Maidan Protests: An Attempt of Systematic Estimation'. *European Politics and Society* 17(4): 453–72. https://doi.org/10.1080/23745118.2016.1154646

Istomin, Igor, and Irina Bolgova. 2016. 'Transnistrian Strategy in the Context of Russian–Ukrainian Relations: The Rise and Failure of "Dual Alignment"'. *Southeast European and Black Sea Studies* 16(1): 169–94. http://dx.doi.org/10.1080/14683857.2016.1148412.

Karagiannis, Emmanuel. 2016. 'Ukrainian Volunteer Fighters in the Eastern Front: Ideas, Political-Social Norms and Emotions as Mobilization Mechanisms'. *Southeast European and Black Sea Studies* 16(1): 139–53. https://doi.org/10.1080/14683857.2016.1148413

Kaufman, Stuart J. 2001. *Modern Hatreds: The Symbolic Politics of Ethnic War*. Ithaka, NY: Cornell University Press.

Kaufmann, Chaim. 1996. 'Possible and Impossible Solutions to Ethnic Civil Wars'. *International Security* 20(4): 136–75.

Kelly, Robert E. 2007. 'Security Theory in the "New Regionalism"'. *International Studies Review* 9(2): 197–229. https://academic.oup.com/isr/article-lookup/doi/10.1111/j.1468-2486.2007.00671.x (September 16, 2018).

Kemp, Walter A. 2014. 'The (Dis)Integration of Moldova? Five Scenarios for Ukraine's Fragile Neighbor'. *IPI Global Observatory*. http://theglobalobservatory.org/2014/05/the-disintegration-of-moldova-five-scenarios-for-ukraines-fragile-neighbor/.

Kennedy, Ryan. 2016. 'The Limits of Soft Balancing: The Frozen Conflict in Transnistria and the Challenge to EU and NATO Strategy'. *Small Wars & Insurgencies* 27(3): 512–37. http://dx.doi.org/10.1080/09592318.2016.1151655.

Kiryukhin, Denys. 2016. 'Russia and Ukraine: The Clash of Conservative Projects'. *European Politics and Society* 17(4): 438–52. http://dx.doi.org/10.1080/2374511 8.2016.1154130.

Konończuk, Wojciech. 2016. 'Ukraine's Omnipresent Oligarchs'. Brussels: Carnegie Europe. http://carnegieeurope.eu/strategiceurope/?fa=64847 (accessed 2 November 2016).

Kortunbov, Andrey. 2017. *Will Donbass Live to See the UN Peacekeepers?* Moscow. http://russiancouncil.ru/en/analytics-and-comments/analytics/will-donbass-live-to-see-the-un-peacekeepers/ (September 15, 2018).

Kroenig, Matthew. 2015. 'Facing Reality: Getting NATO Ready for a New Cold War'. *Survival* 57(1): 49–70. http://dx.doi.org/10.1080/00396338.2015.1008295.

Kubo, Keiichi. 2010. 'Why Kosovar Albanians Took Up Arms against the Serbian Regime: The Genesis and Expansion of the UÇK in Kosovo'. *Europe-Asia Studies* 62(7): 1135–52. www.tandfonline.com/doi/full/10.1080/09668136.2010.4970 22 (September 16, 2018).

Kulyk, Volodymyr. 2016. 'National Identity in Ukraine: Impact of Euromaidan and the War'. *Europe-Asia Studies* 68(4): 588–608. http://dx.doi.org/10.1080/09668 136.2016.1174980.

Lake, David A., and Donald Rothchild. 1996. 'Containing Fear: The Origins and Management of Ethnic Conflict'. *International Security* 21(2): 41–75.

Langer, Arnim. 2015. *When Do Horizontal Inequalities Lead to Conflict? Lessons from a Comparative Study of Ghana and Côte d'Ivoire.* Oxford: Centre for Research on Inequality, Human Security and Ethnicity. www3.qeh.ox.ac.uk/pdf/crisewps/workingpaper82.pdf.

Legvold, Robert. 2014. 'Managing the New Cold War: What Moscow and Washington Can Learn from the Last One'. *Foreign Affairs* 93(4) (July/August): 74–84.

Loshkariov, Ivan D., and Andrey A. Sushentsov. 2016. 'Radicalization of Russians in Ukraine: From "Accidental" Diaspora to Rebel Movement'. *Southeast European and Black Sea Studies* 16(1): 71–90. https://doi.org/10.1080/14683857.2016. 1149349.

Lujala, Päivi, Nils Petter Gleditsch, and Elisabeth Gilmore. 2005. 'A Diamond Curse? Civil War and a Lootable Resource'. *Journal of Conflict Resolution* 49(4): 538–62. http://jcr.sagepub.com/cgi/content/abstract/49/4/538.

Lukin, Alexander. 2014. 'What the Kremlin Is Thinking: Putin's Vision for Eurasia'. *Foreign Affairs* 93(4) (July/August): 85–93.

MacFarlane, Neil, and Anand Menon. 2014. 'The EU and Ukraine'. *Survival* 56(3): 95–101. http://dx.doi.org/10.1080/00396338.2014.920139.

Malyarenko, Tatyana. 2015. 'Playing a Give-Away Game? The Undeclared Russian-Ukrainian War in Donbas'. *Small Wars Journal* 11(12). http://smallwarsjournal.com/jrnl/art/playing-a-give-away-game-the-undeclared-russian-ukrainian-war-in-donbas.

Malyarenko, Tatyana, and David J. Galbreath. 2016. 'Paramilitary Motivation in Ukraine: Beyond Integration and Abolition'. *Southeast European and Black Sea Studies* 16(1): 113–38. http://dx.doi.org/10.1080/14683857.2016.1148414.

Malyarenko, Tatyana, and Stefan Wolff. 2018. 'The Logic of Competitive Influence-Seeking: Russia, Ukraine, and the Conflict in Donbas'. *Post-Soviet Affairs* 34(4): 191–212. www.tandfonline.com/doi/full/10.1080/1060586X.2018.1425083.

Marc, Alexandre, Alys Willman, Ghazia Aslam, Michelle Rebosio, and Kanish-kaa Balasuriya. 2013. *Societal Dynamics and Fragility: Engaging Societies in Responding to Fragile Situations*. Washington, DC: The World Bank Group. https://openknowledge.worldbank.org/handle/10986/12222.

Markedonov, Sergey. 2014. 'Recognition Is Not a Dogma'. *Russia in Global Affairs* 13(4).

———. 2015. 'De Facto Statehood in Eurasia: A Political and Security Phenom-enon'. *Caucasus Survey* 3(3): 195–206. www.tandfonline.com/doi/full/10.1080/2 3761199.2015.1086565 (September 16, 2018).

Marples, David R. 2016. 'Russia's Perceptions of Ukraine: Euromaidan and Histori-cal Conflicts'. *European Politics and Society* 17(4): 424–37. http://dx.doi.org/10. 1080/23745118.2016.1154129.

Matveeva, Anna. 2016. 'No Moscow Stooges: Identity Polarization and Guerrilla Movements in Donbass'. *Southeast European and Black Sea Studies* 16(1): 25–50. https://doi.org/10.1080/14683857.2016.1148415

McFaul, Michael, Stephen Sestanovich, and Stephen Sestanovich. 2014. 'Faulty Powers: Who Started the Ukraine Crisis'. *Foreign Affairs* 93(6) (November/December): 167–78.

McGarry, John, Brendan O'Leary, and Richard Simeon. 2008. 'Integration or Accommodation? The Enduring Debate in Conflict Regulation'. In *Constitutional Design for Divided Societies: Integration or Accommodation*, ed. Sujit Choudhry. Oxford: Oxford University Press, 41–88.

Mearsheimer, John J. 2014. 'Why the Ukraine Crisis Is the West's Fault: The Liberal Delusions That Provoked Putin'. *Foreign Affairs* 93(5) (September/October): 77–89.

Melnyk, Oleksiy, and Andreas Umland. 2016. *Beyond the Minsk Agreements*. Lon-don. www.ecfr.eu/article/commentary_beyond_the_minsk_agreements (Septem-ber 15, 2018).

Mengisteab, Kidane. 2003. 'Africa's Intrastate Conflicts: Relevance and Limitations of Diplomacy'. *African Issues* 31/32: 25–39. www.jstor.org/stable/1535098.

Mikheeva, Oksana. 2014. 'Сучасні Українські Внутрішньо Переміщені Особи: Основні Причини, Стратегії Переселення Та Проблеми Адаптації (Internally Displaced Persons in Contemporary Ukraine: Principal Motivations, Resettle-ment Strategies, and Problems of Adaptation)'. In *Стратегії Трансформації і Превенції Прикордонних Конфліктів в Україні (Transformation Strategy and Prevention of Border Conflicts in Ukraine)*, ed. Nataliya Zubar and Oleg Miro-shnichenko. Lviv: Galician Publishing Association, 9–49. http://peace.in.ua/wp-content/uploads/2016/02/умш-велика-книга.pdf.

———. 2015. *Homo Militans: Війна На Сході України в Оцінках Представників Добровольчих Збройних Формувань – Головні Результати (Homo Militans: In-Depth Interviews with Voluntary Participants of Military Operations in the East of Ukraine – Main Findings)*. Kyiv: Ukrainian Peacebuilding School and British Embassy Kyiv. http://sociology.ucu.edu.ua/wp-content/uploads/2015/12/homo_militans_pressrelease.pdf.

Molchanov, Mikhail A. 2016. 'Choosing Europe over Russia: What Has Ukraine Gained?' *European Politics and Society* 17(4): 522–37. https://doi.org/10.1080/23745118.2016.1154236

Murshed, S. Mansoob, and Scott Gates. 2005. 'Spatial–Horizontal Inequality and the Maoist Insurgency in Nepal'. *Review of Development Economics* 9(1): 121–34. http://dx.doi.org/10.1111/j.1467-9361.2005.00267.x.

Nagashima, Toru. 2017. 'Russia's Passportization Policy toward Unrecognized Republics'. *Problems of Post-Communism*: 1–14. www.tandfonline.com/doi/ful l/10.1080/10758216.2017.1388182 (August 28, 2018).

Neudorfer, Natascha S., and Ulrike G. Theuerkauf. 2014. 'Buying War Not Peace'. *Comparative Political Studies* 47(13): 1856–86. http://journals.sagepub.com/doi/10.1177/0010414013516919 (September 16, 2018).

Nilsson, Martin, and Daniel Silander. 2016. 'Democracy and Security in the EU's Eastern Neighborhood? Assessing the ENP in Georgia, Moldova, and Ukraine'. *Democracy and Security* 12(1): 44–61. http://dx.doi.org/10.1080/17419166.201 5.1135744.

Nitoiu, Cristian. 2016. 'Russia and the EU's Quest for Status: The Path to Conflict in the Post-Soviet Space'. *Global Affairs* 2(2): 143–53. http://dx.doi.org/10.1080 /23340460.2016.1163775.

Norberg, Johan, and Fredrik Westerlund. 2014. *RUFS Briefing Russia and Ukraine: Military-Strategic Options, and Possible Risks, for Moscow*. Stockholm: Swedish Defence Research Agency.

Nováky, Niklas I. M. 2015. 'Why so Soft? The European Union in Ukraine'. *Contemporary Security Policy* 36(2): 244–66. http://dx.doi.org/10.1080/13523260.2 015.1061767.

Oberschall, Anthony. 2000. 'The Manipulation of Ethnicity: From Ethnic Cooperation to Violence and War in Yugoslavia'. *Ethnic and Racial Studies* 23(6): 982–1001. www.tandfonline.com/doi/abs/10.1080/014198700750018388 (June 23, 2018).

Onuch, Olga, and Gwendolyn Sasse. 2016. 'The Maidan in Movement: Diversity and the Cycles of Protest'. *Europe-Asia Studies* 68(4): 556–587. https://doi.org/10.1080/09668136.2016.1159665.

Østby, Gudrun, Henrik Urdal, Mohammad Zulfan Tadjoeddin, S Mansoob Murshed, and Håvard Strand. 2011. 'Population Pressure, Horizontal Inequality and Political Violence: A Disaggregated Study of Indonesian Provinces, 1990–2003'. *The Journal of Development Studies* 47(3): 377–98. http://dx.doi.org/10.1080/00220 388.2010.506911.

Østby, Gudrun, Ragnhild Nordås, and Jan Ketil Rød. 2009. 'Regional Inequalities and Civil Conflict in Sub-Saharan Africa'. *International Studies Quarterly* 53(2): 301–24. http://dx.doi.org/10.1111/j.1468-2478.2009.00535.x.

OTR Online. 2017. 'Александр Гущин: Эскалация Конфликта в Донбассе Говорит о Том, Что в Мирном Процессе До Политического Решения Еще Очень и Очень Далеко (Alexander Gushchin: The Escalation of the Conflict in the Donbass Indicates That We Are Still Very, Very Far Away From)'. https://otr-online.ru/programmi/sotsialnii-reportazh-/situatsiya-na-ukraine-64944.html.

Parks, Thomas, Nat Colletta, and Ben Oppenheim. 2013. *The Contested Corners of Asia: Subnational Conflict and Development Assistance*. San Francisco, CA: The Asia Foundation.

Pinchuk, Andrey. (2017). Тайная война. Во главе министерства госбезопасности ДНР. Moscow: Литпрес. Available at: http://avidreaders.ru/read-book/taynaya-voyna-vo-glave-ministerstva-gosbezopasnosti.html (accessed 2 November 2018).

Posen, Barry R. 1993. 'The Security Dilemma and Ethnic Conflict'. *Survival* 35(1): 27–47. www.tandfonline.com/doi/abs/10.1080/00396339308442672 (June 23, 2018).

Redman, Nicholas. 2014. 'Russia's Breaking Point'. *Survival* 56(2): 235–44. http://dx.doi.org/10.1080/00396338.2014.901781.

Robinson, Paul. 2016. 'Russia's Role in the War in Donbass, and the Threat to European Security'. *European Politics and Society* 17(4): 506–21. https://doi.org/10.1080/23745118.2016.1154229

Rose, William. 2000. 'The Security Dilemma and Ethnic Conflict: Some New Hypotheses'. *Security Studies* 9(4): 1–51. www.tandfonline.com/doi/abs/10.1080/09636410008429412 (June 23, 2018).

Rublee, Maria Rost. 2015. 'Fantasy Counterfactual: A Nuclear-Armed Ukraine'. *Survival* 57(2): 145–56. http://dx.doi.org/10.1080/00396338.2015.1026091.

Rwantabagu, Hermenegilde. 2001. 'Explaining Intra-State Conflicts in Africa: The Case of Burundi'. *International Journal on World Peace* 18(2): 41–53. www.jstor.org/stable/20753302 (September 16, 2018).

Sakwa, Richard 2008. '"New Cold War" or Twenty Years' Crisis? Russia and International Politics'. *International Affairs* 84(2): 241–+.

Salehyan, Idean. 2007. 'Transnational Rebels: Neighboring States as Sanctuary for Rebel Groups'. *World Politics* 59(2): 217–42. www.journals.cambridge.org/abstract_S0043887100020797 (September 16, 2018).

Sambanis, Nicholas. 2001. 'Do Ethnic and Nonethnic Civil Wars Have the Same Causes? A Theoretical and Empirical Inquiry (Part 1)'. *Journal of Conflict Resolution* 45(3): 259–82.

Sasse, Gwendolyn. 2009. 'The European Neighbourhood Policy and Conflict Management: A Comparison of Moldova and the Caucasus'. *Ethnopolitics* 8(3): 369–86. www.informaworld.com/10.1080/17449050903086971.

Schneckener, Ulrich. 2016. 'Hybrider Krieg in Zeiten der Geopolitik? Zur Deutung und Charakterisierung des Donbass-Konflikt'. *PVS Politische Vierteljahresschrift* 57(4): 586–613. http://dx.doi.org/10.5771/0032-3470-2016-4-586.

Siroky, David S., and John Cuffe. 2014. 'Lost Autonomy, Nationalism and Separatism'. *Comparative Political Studies*. http://cps.sagepub.com/content/early/2014/01/29/0010414013516927.abstract.

Smith, Nicholas Ross. 2015. 'The EU and Russia's Conflicting Regime Preferences in Ukraine: Assessing Regime Promotion Strategies in the Scope of the Ukraine Crisis'. *European Security* 24(4): 525–40. http://dx.doi.org/10.1080/09662839.2015.1027768.

Sotiriou, Stylianos A. 2016. 'The Irreversibility of History: The Case of the Ukrainian Crisis (2013–2015)'. *Southeast European and Black Sea Studies* 16(1): 51–70. https://doi.org/10.1080/14683857.2016.1150700.

Stewart, Frances. 2010. *Horizontal Inequalities as a Cause of Conflict: A Review of CRISE Findings*. Oxford: Centre for Research on Inequality, Human Security and Ethnicity.

Strasheim, Julia. 2016. 'Power-Sharing, Commitment Problems, and Armed Conflict in Ukraine'. *Civil Wars*: 1–20. http://dx.doi.org/10.1080/13698249.2016.1 144494.

Theuerkauf, Ulrike G. 2010a. 'Institutional Design and Ethnic Violence: Do Grievances Help to Explain Ethnopolitical Instability?'. *Civil Wars* 12(1–2): 117–39.

———. 2010b. 'Institutional Design and Ethnic Violence: Do Grievances Help to Explain Ethnopolitical Instability?'. *Civil Wars* 12(1–2): 117–39. http://dx.doi.org /10.1080/13698249.2010.486121.

Tolstrup, Jakob. 2015. 'Black Knights and Elections in Authoritarian Regimes: Why and How Russia Supports Authoritarian Incumbents in Post-Soviet States'. *European Journal of Political Research*: n/a-n/a. http://dx.doi.org/10.1111/1475-6765.12079.

UkrlifeTV. 2017. 'Video Interview Igor Todorov: Donbas Will Not Become a New Transnistria'. www.youtube.com/watch?v=JEcGIlGwOz0.

Umland, Andreas. 2018. *UN Peacekeeping in Donbas? The Stakes of the Russia-Ukraine Conflict*. London. www.ecfr.eu/article/commentary_un_peacekeeping_in_donbas_the_stakes_of_the_russia_ukraine_confl (September 15, 2018).

Van Evera, Stephen. 1994. 'Hypotheses on Nationalism and War'. *International Security* 18(4): 5–39. https://muse.jhu.edu/article/447095/summary (September 16, 2018).

Vershbow, Alexander. 2018. *How to Bring Peace to the Donbas*. Washington, DC. www.atlanticcouncil.org/blogs/ukrainealert/how-to-bring-peace-to-the-donbas-yes-it-s-possible (September 15, 2018).

Vieira, Alena Vysotskaya Guedes. 2016. 'Eurasian Integration: Elite Perspectives before and after the Ukraine Crisis'. *Post-Soviet Affairs* 32(6): 566–80. http:// dx.doi.org/10.1080/1060586X.2015.1118200.

Weidmann, Nils B. 2009. 'Geography as Motivation and Opportunity: Group Concentration and Ethnic Conflict'. *Journal of Conflict Resolution* 53(4): 526–43. http://jcr.sagepub.com/content/53/4/526.abstract.

Wilson, Andrew. 2016. 'The Donbas in 2014: Explaining Civil Conflict Perhaps, but Not Civil War'. *Europe-Asia Studies* 68(4): 631–52. http://dx.doi.org/10.1080/0 9668136.2016.1176994.

Wischnath, Gerdis, and Halvard Buhaug. 2014. 'Rice or Riots: On Food Production and Conflict Severity across India'. *Political Geography* 43: 6–15.

Wolff, Andrew T. 2015. 'The Future of NATO Enlargement after the Ukraine Crisis'. *International Affairs* 91(5): 1103–21. http://dx.doi.org/10.1111/1468-2346.12400.

Wolff, Stefan 2011a. 'Managing Ethno-National Conflict: Towards an Analytical Framework'. *Commonwealth and Comparative Politics* 49(2).

———. 2013. 'Conflict Management in Divided Societies: The Many Uses of Territorial Self-Governance'. *International Journal on Minority and Group Rights* 20(1): 27–50. http://booksandjournals.brillonline.com/content/journals/ 10.1163/15718115-02001003.

Wolff, Stefan, and Christalla Yakinthou. 2013. *Conflict Management in Divided Societies: Theories and Practice*.

Wolff, Stefan. 2003. *The German Question since 1919: An Analysis with Key Documents*. Westport, CT: Praeger. https://books.google.co.uk/books/about/The_German_Question_Since_1919.html?id=7aRRFdOSpn0C&redir_esc=y (September 16, 2018).

———. 2011b. 'The Regional Dimensions of State Failure'. *Review of International Studies* 37(3): 951–72. http://dx.doi.org/10.1017/S0260210510000951.

Yost, David S. 2015. 'The Budapest Memorandum and Russia's Intervention in Ukraine'. *International Affairs* 91(3): 505–38. http://dx.doi.org/10.1111/1468-2346.12279.

Yurgens, Igor. 2015. 'A Positive Stalemate for Ukraine'. *Survival* 57(1): 71–77. http://dx.doi.org/10.1080/00396338.2015.1008296.

Zannier, Lamberto. 2015. 'Ukraine and the Crisis of European Security'. *Horizons* 2(2): 44–59. www.cirsd.org/en/horizons/horizons-winter-2015-issue-no2/ukraine-and-the-crisis-of-european-security.

Appendix

List of interviews

Date	Place	Anonymization	Reference
7 May 2014	Donetsk	Senior DPR official	Interview 1
13 June 2014	Donetsk	Senior DPR official	Interview 2
4 July 2014	Donetsk	Senior DPR official	Interview 3
5 July 2014	Donetsk	Senior DPR official	Interview 4
3 August 2014	Donetsk	Senior DPR official	Interview 5
3 August 2014	Donetsk	Senior DPR official	Interview 6
14 September 2015	Kramatorsk	Donetsk state regional administration official	Interview 7
14 September 2015	Kramatorsk	Donetsk state regional administration official	Interview 8
15 September 2015	Kramatorsk	Donetsk state regional administration official	Interview 9
24 September 2015	Mariupol	Former member of 'Dnepr-1' battalion, Ministry of Internal Affairs	Interview 10
24 September 2015	Mariupol	Academic, Donetsk State University of Management	Interview 11
27 November 2015	Vienna	OSCE official	Interview 12
14 January 2016	Washington, D.C.	World Bank official	Interview 13
30 March 2016	Kyiv	EU official	Interview 14
30 March 2016	Kyiv	EU official	Interview 15
30 March 2016	Kyiv	World Bank official	Interview 16
30 March 2016	Kyiv	World Bank official	Interview 17
30 March 2016	Kyiv	World Bank official	Interview 18
1 April 2016	Kyiv	Ukraine Confidence Building Initiative	Interview 19
1 April 2016	Kyiv	Ukraine Confidence Building Initiative	Interview 20

(*Continued*)

(Continued)

Date	Place	Anonymization	Reference
1 April 2016	Kyiv	UNDP official	Interview 21
1 April 2016	Kyiv	OSCE official	Interview 22
1 April 2016	Kyiv	OSCE official	Interview 23
1 April 2016	Kyiv	OSCE official	Interview 24
2 April 2016	Kyiv	Academic, Ukrainian Catholic University, Lviv	Interview 25
6 April 2016	Kyiv	Former Ukrainian MP	Interview 26
6 April 2016	Kyiv	Human rights activist	Interview 27
7 April 2016	e-mail	Advisor, Russian Council on International Affairs	Interview 28
9 April 2016	e-mail	Advisor, Russian Council on International Affairs	Interview 29
13 April 2016	e-mail	Academic, Financial University under the Government of the Russian Federation	Interview 30
13 April 2016	e-mail	Academic, Perm State University	Interview 31
15 April 2016	Chisinau	ECMI Ukraine representative	Interview 32
29 April 2016	Kyiv	Ukrainian NGO activist	Interview 33
29 April 2016	Kyiv	Ukrainian Helsinki Human Rights Union official	Interview 34
3 May 2016	e-mail	Representative, Gorchakov Foundation	Interview 35
17 June 2016	e-mail	Representative, US-Russia Business Council, Eurasia Foundation	Interview 36
18 September 2016	e-mail	Representative, Carnegie Moscow Center	Interview 37
29 September 2016	e-mail	Academic, Southern Federal University	Interview 38
29 September 2016	e-mail	Academic, Southern Federal University	Interview 39
1 October 2016	e-mail	Academic, MGIMO	Interview 40
10 April 2017	Kyiv	NGO, Institute for Peace	Interview 41
11 April 2017	Kyiv	Colonel (ret.), Ukrainian Armed Forces	Interview 42
11 April 2017	Kyiv	Major General (ret.), Ukrainian Armed Forces	Interview 43
12 April 2017	Kyiv	UNDP, Kramatorsk-Donetsk	Interview 44
12 April 2017	Kyiv	Academic, Boris Grinchenko University, IDP from Donetsk	Interview 45
18 April 2017	Kramatorsk	Journalist, IDP from Donetsk	Interview 46

Date	Place	Anonymization	Reference
18 April 2017	Kramatorsk	UNICEF, Kramatorsk, IDP from Luhansk	Interview 47
12 April 2017	Kyiv	Academic, Kyiv Boris Grinchenko University, IDP from Donetsk	Interview 48
28 April 2017	Kyiv	Academic, National University 'Kyiv Mohyla Academy'	Interview 49
28 April 2017	Kyiv	Journalist, researcher on decentralisation reform	Interview 50
29 April 2017	Kharkiv	Academic, 'Karazin Kharkiv National University'	Interview 51
29 April 2017	Kharkiv	Academic and NGO, 'Karazin Kharkiv National University'	Interview 52
4 May 2017	Skype	Head of Information Policy Department, Poltava State Regional Administration	Interview 53
6 May 2017	Skype	Deputy of local municipality, Uzhgorod	Interview 54
18 May 2017	Skype	Academic, Head of Ukraine-NATP Centre in Uzhgorod National University, IDP from Donetsk	Interview 55
2 July 2017	Mariupol	Former deputy head of Donetsk city administration	Interview 56
2 July 2017	Mariupol	Former head of local administration of a city district in Donetsk	Interview 57
6 August 2017	Kyiv	Former deputy minister, Government of Ukraine	Interview 58
7 August 2017	Kyiv	Former minister, Government of Ukraine	Interview 59
7 August 2017	Kyiv	Former member of Parliament of Ukraine	Interview 60
8 August 2017	Kyiv	Former member of Parliament of Ukraine	Interview 61
30 August 2017	Skype	Former member of Luhansk regional council	Interview 62
30 August 2017	Odessa	Former member of Parliament of Ukraine	Interview 63
30 August 2017	Odessa	Former head of Odessa regional council	Interview 64
31 August 2018	Skype	Donetsk-based civil society activist	Interview 65

List of workshops

Workshop Date	Workshop Place	Workshop Title	Participants Anonymization	Reference
14–22 May 2014	Kyiv	'Enhancing Strategic Analytical Capabilities in NATO Partner Countries: Security Cooperation and the Management of Current and Future Threats in Europe's Strategic Orbit'	Civilian and military experts from various research institutions, think tanks, international organisations, NATO international military staff	Workshop A
29 February 2015	Rome, NATO Defence College	'Ukraine and Its Neighbourhood: How to Deal with Aggressive Russia'	Civilian and military experts from various research institutions, think tanks, international organisations, NATO international military staff	Workshop B
29–30 April 2015	Rome, NATO Defence College	'NATO and New Ways of Warfare: Defeating Hybrid Threats'	Civilian and military experts from various research institutions, think tanks, international organisations, NATO onternational military staff	Workshop C
26–27 August 2015	Kyiv	'Minorities and the Construction of an Inclusive Society: Ukraine, Moldova and National Practice'	Ukrainian and Moldovan government representatives, representatives of Ukrainian and Moldovan NGOs	Workshop D
21 September 2015	Washington, D.C., George Marshall Plan Foundation	'U.S. and European Russia Policy: Toward a Strategy'	Civilian and military experts from various research institutions, think tanks, international organisations, NATO international military staff	Workshop E

23–24 November 2015	Chisinau	'Minorities and the Construction of an Inclusive Society: Moldova, Ukraine and International Practice'	Ukrainian and Moldovan government representatives, OSCE, EU officials, officials from local embassies, representatives of Ukrainian and Moldovan NGOs	Workshop F
2 December 2015	Washington, D.C., George Marshall Plan Foundation	'Russia's Long War on Ukraine'	Civilian and military experts from various research institutions, think tanks, international organisations, NATO international military staff	Workshop G
15–16 December 2015	Washington, D.C., John Hopkins University, Supreme Allied Commander Transformation	'NATO Transformation and Adaptation'	Civilian and military experts from various research institutions, think tanks, international organisations, NATO international military staff	Workshop H
24–25 February 2016	Kyiv	'Conflict in Ukraine and the Road Ahead: Impacts on Livelihoods and Development Prospects'	Ukrainian government representatives, OSCE, EU, UN and World Bank representatives, representatives from local embassies, representatives of Ukrainian NGOs	Workshop I
1–2 April 2016	Kyiv	'Strengthening Democratic Security Governance in the European Union's Neighbourhood'	Experts, analysts from governmental, non-governmental and academic institutions in Bulgaria, France, Italy, Latvia, Moldova, Poland, UK, Ukraine, US	Workshop J

(Continued)

(Continued)

Workshop Date	Workshop Place	Workshop Title	Participants Anonymization	Reference
27 April 2016	Washington, D.C., John Hopkins University, Supreme Allied Commander Transformation	'NATO's Future: Bigger and Better or Tired and Torn?'	Civilian and military experts from various research institutions, think tanks, international organisations, NATO international military staff	Workshop K
10–12 April 2017	Kyiv	'The EU's Comprehensive Approach to Security in the Eastern Neighbourhood'	Civilian and military experts from various research institutions, think tanks, the EU, and the Ukrainian government	Workshop L
17–19 September 2017	Odessa	'The EU and International Conflicts: Current and Future Developments to Improve European Crisis Management and Conflict Prevention in Fragile and Conflict-Affected Countries'	Civilian and military experts from various research institutions, think tanks, the EU, and the Ukrainian government	Workshop M

Index

For Product Safety Concerns and Information please contact our EU
representative GPSR@taylorandfrancis.com
Taylor & Francis Verlag GmbH, Kaufingerstraße 24, 80331 München, Germany